FINDING THE RIGHT DOOR

A Realtor's Perspective

ANGELA D. BEAN

Finding The Right Door
By Angela D. Bean

ISBN 978-0-578-89249-8

Unless otherwise indicated, all Scripture quotations in this book are taken from the King James Version (KJV) of the Holy Bible.

Disclaimer: The advice, opinions, and strategies contained herein may not be suitable for every situation. This work is sold with the understanding that the Author and Publisher are not engaged in rendering legal, emotional, spiritual, or other professional services or advice.

Edited by: Fiverr Pro

Printed in the United States of America

Published by: Angela D. Bean

Published in the United States of America

ACKNOWLEDGMENT

Thank you to the Realtors who serve with integrity as they assist their clients through the process of finding The Right Door.

Dedicated to my clients for trusting me as their Realtor to assist them in finding their Right Door during one of the most pivotal times in their lives.

"God opens *doors* that no man can shut, and he shuts *doors* that no man can open" (Revelation 3:7). God is the *door*keeper. Don't allow the wrong door to keep you from your purpose. Obstacles can't stop what God has ordained for you when you walk through the Right Door.

TABLE OF CONTENTS

INTRODUCTION

This book is about finding your *Right Door.* It is about the *integrity* of the Realtor's relationships with their peers and their clients. It is about *faith* and how to apply it throughout your journey while finding the Right Door. It is also about unraveling the mysteries behind the scenes that cause fear and anxiety while finding the Right Door. Although this book is told from a Realtor's perspective, you will find that you can apply some of the same principles to other life situations, such as finding the right job, the right investments, the right relationships, the right mate, and the list goes on. Most times, in our quest to find the Right Door, we are presented with choices. Choosing the Right Door is imperative for our well-being. It's essential to be where God wants us to be so that He can use us for the purpose He has intended, without hindrances. We are talking about the Right Door, not the perfect door. Because our lives are forever changing, we will experience more than one Right Door; however, choosing the Right Door at the right time is key. In Real Estate, you will know that you have selected the Right Door when you walk through it the first time, you will sleep that night free from worry and anxiety, you will have inner peace, and you will be filled with the hope that your offer will get accepted.

There were times when I have shown a house to a client, and they knew they were home when they first walked through the door. Although the physical, which was tangible, was pleasing, there was always an intangible feeling that let them know they were home. It is a gut feeling, where the Holy Spirit is witnessing, to them, that they just walked through the Right Door, the place they would call home.

My objective is to help the reader understand the general process of the real estate transaction, from the offer to the closing, from my perspective and experiences. Understanding and knowing the process should help reduce the mystery that tends to cause fear and anxiety during the silent time when you are waiting to hear a favorable decision from the other party. Fear can manifest itself in many ways, including lack of control over a situation, the unknown, and the hidden things that lurk in the darkness (the mystery). Therefore, shining light on the process will help eliminate, or at least reduce, the fear and anxiety. However, I can't talk about any of those things without including faith and patience. Whether you're the client or the agent, it would be beneficial to have some faith as you go through this process because faith ensues patience. Having faith and patience can reduce and even eliminate anxiety and fear.

I will also talk about the integrity and ethical morals required in the agent's relationships with their clients, fellow agents, and others involved in the transaction process.

I chose to tell seven of my clients' stories and their journeys in finding their Right Door. Although "time is of the essence" is prevalent in the real estate arena, their stories give a whole new meaning to that phrase. You will notice how each client experienced a personal dilemma while going through the stress of relocation. You will see how "time" was a significant factor in their dilemma. You will also see that, despite their dilemma, each client found their Right Door.

After many years of watching my clients experience worry and concern as I responded to their questions and helped them through the process, I decided to document my knowledge using an analogy familiar to most, the amusement park. A specific amusement park ride represents each client's journey.

MY STORY

Faith

Definition:

1. **"Something that is believed especially with strong conviction" (*Merriam-Webster Dictionary*).**
2. **"Now faith is the substance of things hoped for, the evidence of things not seen" (Hebrews 11:1 KJV).**

Faith is essential to have when looking for the Right Door; without that, it can lead to uncertainty and doubt, which can cause fear and anxiety, which is the opposite of faith. This is what I experienced in my early years of selling real estate. In the beginning, I thought each case would be similar to the other, but I soon found out that was not so. Each case was uniquely and inevitably different because I dealt with different people and different sets of circumstances.

At some point, throughout the real estate transaction process, a lack of faith would allow doubt and anxiety to enter in for both the client and me. The level of faith I thought I had was revealed during the silent period of the process, which could occur at any time, from expectation to manifestation (offer to closing). Just attending church and learning about faith was not growing my faith; it was increasing my knowledge. It is through our experiences, tests, trials, and tribulations where our faith grows. We must put in the work during the difficult and uncertain times and not give up if we want to continue to grow in our faith. *Faith without works is also dead* (James 2:26). If the process produced the same or similar results each time, it would be familiar and predictable and easy to say I have faith because I would have already known the outcome; this was how I used to measure my faith. However, if every outcome were familiar and predictable, it would have been impossible for my faith to increase. God does not reveal everything to us at one time. He wants us to have faith and know that He's working it out, even when we don't understand how, when, or why. He just asks us to have faith and patience and to trust in Him. True faith exists when we trust and know, without a doubt, that God is working things out.

> *It is through our experiences, tests, trials, and tribulations where our faith grows. We must put in the work during the difficult and uncertain times and not give up if we want to continue to grow in our faith. Faith without works is also dead (James 2:26).*

Throughout the years, and after several transactions, my faith has, inevitably, increased. It was not immediate; I had to go through the journey of experiencing several different transactions. As I mentioned earlier, each transaction's journey and process are uniquely different—it's never predictable or the same. Sometimes the uncertainty occurred at the beginning, the middle, or at the end of the transaction. I have learned that my faith would not have increased if the outcome was the same or predictable each time. Although challenging and frustrating at times, I'm glad I didn't quit or give up but instead allowed this experience to help me grow in my faith, not just in real estate transactions but also in life. I learned that sometimes we could become too comfortable and complacent in our lives and stop growing and discovering where we lack. God's purpose for us is continuous until the end. We are vessels chosen to do God's work on earth; therefore, He wants us to continue to grow in knowledge, wisdom, and faith so that He can continue to use us through our assignments. When God gives us an assignment, we should not avoid it but rather allow the challenge to grow us in areas of our lives where we lack so that we can be promoted to the next assignment.

True faith exists when we trust and know, without a doubt, that God is working things out. I can't predict the exact outcome of each of my cases, but by faith, I know that "in the end, it is all going to work out." And this is what I now tell my clients.

> *True faith exists when we trust and know, without a doubt, that God is working things out.*

Assignments

Selling real estate is a journey where ministry, integrity, prayer, and faith are part of that journey. Whenever we encounter others, there is an opportunity to minister (it's inevitable) because of our purpose here, on earth. **Each of us has a purpose (it's why we exist); we did not show up on this earth just to eat, drink and be merry.** Some of our parents may not have planned for us, but God knew us and had a purpose and plan for our lives before we were even in our mother's womb (Jeremiah 1:5). He gave each of us gifts to carry out our purpose through our assignments. Some of those gifts are obvious, such as teaching and public speaking, music and the arts, science and medicine, helping and serving, and the list goes on. However, many people do not know or recognize their gifts because they are not as obvious, but we each have at least one gift. Even though your gift may not be obvious, your purpose is not less important than anyone else's. One thing for sure is that our purpose always has to do with making a difference in the lives of others. Therefore, our call is significant and needed for God's Kingdom. Whatever our gift(s) is, it is not just for our well-being, but also to impact others by assisting them in the areas where they may have a void or lack—just as we benefit from the gifts of others to help complete us in the areas where we may lack. Like a chain-link fence, we are all connected to make a whole.

Discovering your gifts is not difficult or a mystery—you can discover them through what you do naturally and through your personality. Each of us has a unique personality. There is no other person with your exact personality; they might have similar personalities, but not the exact one. We are unique individuals, fearfully and wonderfully made. So, wherever you are, and whatever you're doing, do it for the ministry of God. It could be as simple as a smile or a greeting; right there, you just impacted someone. You never know what someone is going through, and sowing that seed of kindness may have been just what that person needed at that moment.

We are unique individuals, fearfully and wonderfully made.

Money, an event, that special someone, and life pleasures may fulfill us for a moment or a season, but nothing can fulfill and sustain us, in the long run, as living our lives on purpose by sharing our gifts. It's our ministry. The saying, "It's better to give than to receive," is true; you would have to experience it to realize it. "*Look not every man on his own things, but every man also on the things of others" (Philippians 2:4).*

God gives us assignments throughout our lives; these assignments relate to our purpose. Some assignments are short-term, and some are long-term. Some are general, and some are specific. I have heard many interpretations and explanations regarding our purpose and assignments. The following is my interpretation: My *general* purpose is to win souls to God's Kingdom (Matthew 28:19-20). My *specific* purpose is to be a vessel that God uses to do His work on earth, through my assignments, with how I impact others with my God-given gifts, talents, knowledge, experiences, and abilities. However we interpret our purpose, the key is to be obedient when God gives us an assignment so we can live a purpose-filled life.

There are many reasons why someone might choose to avoid their assignments, including the following: Some will avoid their assignment because they don't feel qualified, worthy, or strong enough to carry out the assignment; this generally is based on a lack of confidence and faith. Then, there are those who have carried out their assignment and made mistakes then try to cover it up with deception; and finally, those who, because of their quest for perfection, are afraid of making mistakes; therefore, they choose not to do the assignment at all. The latter two can lead to pride, and as we all know, pride is destructive on so many levels. In one of his Daily Devotions, Bishop Keith A. Butler explains it like this:

"Pride convinces us that we need to display an image of perfection to be strong. Therefore, we often won't admit when we've done wrong, or we don't give a sincere apology. It takes a strong individual to admit when they were wrong'.

"How can we be strong enough to walk out our purpose with power? Paul wrote to Timothy that he must be strong in the grace that comes from Christ Jesus. It is in this grace that the weak say I am strong (Joel 3:10). His grace is not weak; it is the supernatural power of God. God gives this strength of grace to the humble (James 4:6)".

Good stewards are given more assignments along with the accompanying ability and anointing to achieve them.

Therefore, when God gives us assignments, we should not avoid them because, through our assignments, our growth occurs, allowing God to elevate and promote us to more awesome assignments.

God has given me many assignments in my lifetime and will continue to do so. Some of those assignments I have fulfilled and some I have avoided. For instance, this book, which I have delayed writing for several years, not because of pride but because I'm not a "writer." Also, I didn't think it would be helpful or interesting enough and, therefore, I didn't want to waste my time. However, that changed after working with several of my clients. I began to see a pattern at the end of the process of how God worked things out. Because of their journeys and experiences in finding their Right Door, several of these clients told me that I need to write a book. As one of my friends put it, "You just can't make this stuff up." I received further confirmation at the 2019 Realtors Conference in San Francisco. The National Association of Realtors (NAR) President stated that every Realtor should be writing a book to tell their stories. (It was good to hear that confirmation because I had already begun writing my book). Throughout my real estate journeys, I experienced how God worked things out for the good. God will give us the desires of our hearts, and all He asks for in return is that we acknowledge Him with our praises and testimonies. **I would be remiss if I did not do *that for Him after all He has done for me and what I have witnessed Him do for others.*** We must share our stories with others because there is always some information that may be useful to someone.

Another one of my assignments is the role of a Realtor. When I decided to become a Realtor, I never thought that my faith would be tested and tested often; and that my prayer life would increase to another level, more specifically interceding in prayer for others. When clients seek Realtors' services, most of the time, they are looking to make significant life changes through relocation. They are also making one of the most significant financial transactions of their lives, and, of course, they are hoping for a successful outcome. They look to us beyond the Realtor's general services; we wear many hats, including counselor, attorney, accountant, and prayer partner.

The nuances of finding the Right Door in a timely manner, the negotiation process, and getting a clear to close can sometimes cause turbulence, leading the client to worry and experience anxiety, especially when pressed for time. It is then that a client might look to their agent for hope. That's where faith and prayer enter in; at that point, it's time to turn up the prayers and stir up the faith. When the client turns to me looking for the super on my natural, I turn it over to God, Jehovah Jireh (my provider), because only He can supernaturally cause the outcome to be a total success. Once the client has found their Right Door, the offer has been submitted, and negotiations have concluded, my job is to get the client to the closing table. This process is not always easy when dealing with several different people and entities; therefore, once I've done all I can do, above and beyond what's required, I turn it over to Jehovah God through prayer. Then, by faith, I am convinced that however it turns out, it was meant to be (even if the deal falls through) because when one door closes, another one opens—the Right Door. I usually tell my clients that at some point in the process, you might experience some turbulence, so strap on your seat belt, buckle up, stir up your faith, pray and try to enjoy the ride; and know that, in the end, it will all work out for your good—you will find your right door, at the right time, for the right price.

The client and the agent must exercise patience, especially through the turbulent period, if they want to come out unscathed without a compromising character. I had to learn this lesson many years ago. Before becoming a real estate agent, I realized that patience was not one of my strengths. We all have strengths and weaknesses, and this was one of my weaknesses. If you want to test the spectrum of your patience, try taking a cake decorating class, where you attempt to make flowers, but the results are unidentifiable objects. So you drop out after the first class (yep, that was me in my 30s). Even at an early age, it seems I was always rushing through life. For example, when I was in high school, my goal was to graduate a year before my time; therefore, I spent two summers attending summer school. There were other instances in my youth that I felt I had to rush through as well. My mother would ask me, "Why are you rushing your life? Slow down!" Another example, both in high school and college, as soon as I received my syllabus, I would begin working on my assignments. The problem with that was sometimes the syllabus would change, and I would end up doing more than one assignment. What am I saying here? Without patience, you can find yourself spinning around on the hamster's wheel, exerting unnecessary effort, time, and energy that could have been better used for something else, like your God-given assignment(s).

I did not discover that my lack of patience was a problem until I began working for the City of Detroit, where I interacted with the public regularly, in person, and by phone. Then, I knew if I wanted to get through a day or a week without getting stressed out, I had to get this problem under control. Lack of patience inevitably affects your faith. Lack of patience can hurt your relationships. Lack of patience usually leads to stress and anxiety, affecting your health, which happened to me.

Because of my lack of patience, I experienced anxiety attacks—although mild, they were uncomfortable. Therefore, to help build and strengthen myself in that area, I researched natural self-improvement techniques. The methods that worked best for me and what I continue to apply are physical and spiritual exercises. Because I'm one of those rare people who (actually) enjoy exercising, I tend to participate in many different forms of it sporadically. However, my regular, daily exercises are walking, yoga and Pilates.

I've been a walker consistently, over thirty years. Walking fortifies me physically, mentally, and spiritually. It helps me alleviate stress and anxiety; it helps me unwind and put things in perspective; it clarifies my thoughts, especially during negotiations (the bumper car, which is discussed later in this book). Walking is therapeutic for me; it is also one of my "prayer closets." After completing my walk, I feel "I can do all things through Christ who strengthens me" (Philippians 4:13 NKJV).

I recently added Pilates and yoga exercises (not the spiritual kind) to my daily exercise routine. The stretching, core strengthening, and breathing techniques from yoga and Pilates are like medicine to the body (it's also easy on the joints). I began doing these two exercises after going to physical therapy for lower back pain. I realized that the exercises the therapist had me performing were similar to the exercises in my yoga and Pilates classes; therefore, I continue to do them daily to ease the back pain and relieve stress.

Typically, my spiritual life consists of daily prayer, praise and worship, and studying the scriptures. Through studying the Word, I found that there are many scriptures on patience. The two that I chose to meditate on were:

> 1) Proverbs 3:5,6 – "Trust in the Lord with all your heart and lean not unto thine own understanding. In all thy ways acknowledge him, and he shall direct thy paths."
>
> 2) Philippians 4:6,7 – "Be anxious for nothing but in everything by prayer and supplication with thanksgiving let your request be made known unto God. And the peace of God, which passeth all understanding, shall keep your hearts and minds through Christ Jesus."

What I realized is that patience and faith go hand in hand. As stated in the book of James 1:3, "…the testing of your faith produces patience." I am not sure if it was age, growing wiser, self-improvement techniques (meditation and exercise), or a combination of them, but I must say (even though I'm a work in progress), I am more patient these days. And when I do feel my patience being tested, I remind myself, "this too shall pass." By the way, lack of patience was not my only flaw. I have other flaws and idiosyncrasies, but it was one of the major flaws that hindered me from showing up at my best when dealing with people and situations.

As Realtors, we encounter many people. While patience may not be the area you lack, I encourage you to find or face the qualities you lack in your personality and character to focus on improvement. Although, because no one is perfect, you may find that you possess more than one flaw, focus on the obvious one (or two) that hinders you from showing up at your best. In my personal and professional life, I have come across many different personality traits and character flaws in people, including but not limited to the following: narcissistic characteristics, impatience, competitive or controlling spirit, too aggressive or too passive, rude, deceptive, impulsive, not a good listener, and the list goes on. Whatever flaw(s) you may have that impairs you from interacting with others effectively, patiently, and compassionately, be honest with yourself and find out how you can overcome them. Do this for yourself, and you will find that it will make your interactions with others more effective. Also, even if we are in denial of our flaws or too afraid to face them, others can see them (clearly), they can feel our energy. I talk about this later in this book, with the house of mirrors analogy.

Although I have worked on my patience, I have a low tolerance for certain things in life; therefore, I have turned down a few assignments that could have rendered very generous commissions. These assignments, I felt, would have either presented a safety issue or there was evidence of fraud. In addition, I have also turned down assignments where I felt the person was not serious about purchasing; they just wanted to ride the merry-go-round, which I also talk about later.

A large part of assisting the client with finding their Right Door has a lot to do with the relationship. Being aware of our shortcomings will help us to experience healthier relationships. This awareness is essential in real estate because most clients are not just buying or selling homes. They are also experiencing other life changes and challenges, which, typically, is the reason that leads them to have to buy or sell their home. Some of these life changes are positive, such as marriage, increase in their family, and job relocation, while some are challenging, such as divorce, death, sickness, and aging. One thing for sure, whether it is a joyous or difficult situation, the bottom line is, the process of moving is stressful in and of itself. Therefore, whenever we encounter our clients, we should do our best not to add to their stress with our shortcomings but always try to show up with a peaceful and joyful spirit.

As Realtors, we are taught or have read books on how to be successful in this profession; however, success is not solely based on how much money we make, but more importantly, on good and healthy relationships. When we treat people well, we feel good. When we put people first, success will follow. (As the Financial Guru, Suze Orman, says, "People first, then money, then things." (I'd like to add, "God first, then people, then money, then things.") Also, most agents will acquire most of their clients through referrals from people they know; therefore, good and healthy relationships are essential to success.

Identifying our weaknesses and shortcomings will help us improve in those areas and become the best person God has created us to be for our own sake, then others will reap its benefits.

Real Estate Experience

I have been in the real estate arena most of my life. Like most little girls, I had a fascination with dollhouses. I had dollhouses that my mother bought me for Christmas and dollhouses that I made from cardboard, and then later, I was excited to purchase dollhouses for my daughter, then for my granddaughters. Lately, one of my favorite pastimes is home tours. My friends and I usually aim for two to four tours each year. I find the architectural style and decor of the homes fascinating and always leave with great decorating ideas. In some cases, I also notice how the decor reflects the homeowner's personality, which I find interesting.

My first steady job, of thirty-one years, was with the City of Detroit, where I spent twenty-six of those years working in the Real Estate and Housing Services Divisions. The last sixteen years of my employment with the City were in the Planning and Development Department's Housing Services Division. I started as a Housing Rehabilitation Program Case Manager. One of my tasks was to approve qualified applicants to participate in various grant programs for housing rehabilitation. I spent the last ten years as a program manager for some of those same programs. At each level, I interacted with the public regularly. In addition, while employed with the City, I owned and operated an appraisal company (part-time) for thirteen years. Those experiences, and my current positions as a Realtor and mobile notary signing agent, are the reasons why I have been inside close to a thousand houses in the Southeast area of the State of Michigan.

I am thankful for my background as a real estate appraiser; it has allowed me to be familiar with most neighborhoods in Michigan's Southeast area, particularly the tri-county area. That knowledge has become my niche in selling real estate by accurately identifying the market value. Typically, realtors would create a comparative market analysis (CMA) to gauge a property's value for their clients. However, because of my appraiser experience, I tend to go beyond the CMA requirements to determine the best listing price for my sellers and my buyers' best offer. The results are close to, and, in some cases, precisely, the appraisal value. The appraisal experience has also allowed me to obtain my real estate broker's license without the required real estate sales experience.

Real estate is not just brick and mortar to me—there is something about assisting people in their housing needs, whether through the home repair programs during my employment with the City government and now as a Realtor. Through my experience with the City government, I have learned that my personality is more of a public servant than a salesperson. Therefore, I've never desired to be in sales and had always said if I find myself selling anything, it had to be something that the person wanted or needed, without me trying to convince them that it was right for them. I always felt that it took too much time and effort to convince someone to settle for something they did not particularly want, need, or could afford. Therefore, in sales, I focus more on assisting and educating others in making their best choice.

Selling is a talent and gift that some possess naturally (I do not naturally possess this gift). These people tend to be great salespersons. There have been many studies on what makes for a great salesperson. The one that stood out to me was the comparison between empathy and ego. This study stated if you possess both qualities, there is a good chance of you becoming a great salesperson. Based on this study, I fall into the empathy category. As stated earlier, I'm not going to persuade or convince anyone to purchase anything but will assist, educate and provide them with the necessary resources and knowledge. However, once they have made a choice, that is when my ego kicks in. I will relentlessly try to get them an acceptable offer.

Once I retired from the City, I knew that I wanted to continue to make a difference by serving others in some capacity; therefore, along with volunteering with my church and various non-profit organizations, I decided to get my real estate license. I knew that this occupation would keep me as busy as I wanted to be and provide me with camaraderie and relationships while providing a service. Because I wanted to enjoy my experience as a Realtor, I decided to do it part-time, giving each client my undivided attention without the stress. My approach as a Realtor is to fulfill my clients' needs by assisting, educating, and providing them with information to make the best choices for themselves. This approach fulfills me because I know from experience that a person's home should bring them peace, comfort, and security, and only they would know when they have found their Right Door.

I must mention it again: Don't allow the commission to be your only incentive to join the real estate profession (or any other profession, for that matter, if you can help it). I guarantee that, eventually, you will have no joy in that alone. In this profession, stress is inevitable because of the constant interactions with others and the uncertainty that comes with it. If you are solely focused on money, you won't last long before becoming consumed with unnecessary, deadly stress, bad habits, and relationships. This profession can also be very emotional (at times) for both the agent and client; therefore, having compassion and patience towards people is a must. Money can provide comfort, security, and temporary happiness, but joy comes when you help others find their happiness and joy. Therefore, always try to choose a profession that aligns with your gifts and talents; that's where you will find the most joy in your performance and relationships, which inevitably will lead to success.

Don't get me wrong—there's nothing wrong with striving to be financially blessed. I desire to be abundantly, financially blessed, as much as the next person. One of my favorite scriptures regarding prosperity and wealth is Malachi 3:10, that as a giver, "the Lord will open up the windows of heaven and pour me out a blessing, that I wouldn't have room enough to receive it." This kind of blessing will grant me the ability to be a blessing to others and still have more than enough to enjoy myself. However, on the flip side, 1st Timothy 6:10 says, "the **Love** of money is the root to all evil." To love it is to make it your god. To love it can cause you to lose your soul. To love, it can cause one to lie, kill, and steal and, inevitably, cause harm to themselves and others. To love, it can affect how we treat others. "For where your treasure is, there will your heart be also" (Matthew 16:21).

Agents should not be a respecter of persons; we should give every client the same respect and attention, whether it's a thousand-dollar-a-month lease or a million-dollar sale. Each client is looking for their Right Door, and therefore, our mission should always be to assist them in finding it. The person looking for a lease is just as important to God as the one looking for a million-dollar house. Their Right Door could be the door where God wants them to be at a specific time in their lives, and, therefore, we should not be the obstacle to prevent this from happening.

Agents should not be a respecter of persons; we should give every client the same respect and attention, rather if it's a thousand-dollar-a-month lease or a million-dollar sale.

In my first year of selling real estate, I had a client looking for a lease. Before working with this client, I just sold a property that yielded me a large commission check. I did not have a personal relationship with either client but gave each one the same professional service as the other. At the closing, the lease client thanked me for taking their case and stated that they were unsuccessful in obtaining an agent before signing on with me.

They stated that when they spoke with other agents about their interest in leasing, the agents never followed up; one agent told them he was busy dealing with purchasers and did not have the time to deal with any lessees. Maybe I'm missing something, but I never thought we measured a person's needs by the size of a commission check.

A good name will last longer than a commission check. **"A good name is rather to be chosen than great riches and loving favor rather than silver and gold" (Proverbs 22:1 KJV).**

THE AMUSEMENT PARK

I chose the amusement park analogy to illustrate the real estate process and journey because it is familiar and relatable to most. Most clients will experience up to four different rides and, sometimes, the fun house-house of mirrors. The Realtor is the park keeper who will experience each ride with the client, some actually and some vicariously. The rides that the client will experience are the merry-go-round, Ferris wheel, roller coaster, and bumper cars. Some might also go through the house of mirrors located in the funhouse. The rides can be fun, exciting, and thrilling if you don't get stuck on them too long or have to ride them repeatedly against your will. If the latter happens, the merry-go-round and Ferris wheel experience can become annoying and frustrating. The roller coaster experience can become daunting, frightening, and filled with dismay. This tends to happen during the "quiet" times (the mystery). Having faith will allow one to know, no matter what it looks like (or doesn't), God is working it all out behind the scenes; He keeps us hidden until it is done.

The amusement park illustration will take you on the journey with the client, from entering the park to exiting (the closing). The journey will help you understand the process and some of the hiccups along the way; it will also help unravel some of the mysteries during the silent periods. Warning: *after reading this, you might never look at the amusement park the same!*

Initial Meeting with the Client

The initial meeting with the client is where the itinerary to the amusement park gets established. In this meeting, the agent and client establish their relationship (who wants to hang out at the park for months with someone without first establishing a relationship based on mutual expectations with one another—, not me). In the meeting, the agent and client usually share general, and personal information about each other, such as family, schools attended, and interests. The agent will ask many questions to gather pertinent information. One of the questions asked is, "What are the client's motive and purpose for deciding to relocate?"

The meeting also determines a course of action, including signing several documents, such as the agency disclosure and other required documents necessary to carry out the assignment. For the buyer, the agent will verify their pre-approval letter and discuss the criteria they are looking for in their future home, including the style, price, location, and amenities. When discussing the criteria, I always ask my clients to specify the "must-haves" and the optional ones. The "must-haves" are what tend to bring them the peace and comfort they're looking for in their home. The goal is to fulfill everything in their criteria; however, that's not always possible for various reasons. The initial meeting with the seller consists of them signing and filling out all required documents necessary to list their property. They will also choose the showing dates and times conducive to their schedule. As a precaution for my clients, I am meticulous with the details of the showing instructions, especially if they plan to occupy the property during the showings.

Now that the agenda has been established, time to head to the park. Before entering the park, I like to inform my clients that, no matter what happens, know that everything will all work out in the end. Stir up your faith because, at some point, you might experience some turbulence, so strap in, buckle up and try to enjoy the rides. Upon entering the park, everyone is full of hope and expectations and is excited and looking forward to the experience. Everything seems bright and colorful; there are games, rides, exhibits, and all the yummy junk food. LET THE ADVENTURE BEGIN!!!

The Merry-Go-Round (Showings)

Merry-Go-Round - Your Dictionary

Carousel: a pleasure ride consisting of a slowly revolving circular platform affixed with various types of seats, frequently horses or other animals, typically found at fairs and amusement parks.

In my first few years as an agent, I encountered a few who were not serious buyers; they just wanted to ride the merry-go-round repeatedly. In other words, they just wanted to go house touring or window shopping, with no intentions of purchasing anything. I now prevent this from happening by requiring proof that they are serious about purchasing. I ask the why, how, and where questions regarding their decision to purchase. I also request proof of their pre-qualification or pre-approval letter from their lender and EMD (earnest money deposit). Having these items proves to me that the buyer is serious about buying. Having these items before searching for a home is beneficial because most offers would not get accepted without a lender's approval letter and proof of the EMD. Also, having these items could expedite the offer's acceptance, which is advantageous in a sellers' market. Therefore, potential buyers who have their approval letter and EMD will move more quickly with a successful offer.

Once I have determined that the buyer is serious and qualified to purchase, I will set up an auto-email on the MLS (multi-listing system) to begin receiving listings that meet their criteria. After the buyer has received several listings containing their criteria, they will select all they want to view. The agent will then schedule the showings. At this point, the agent and client will board the merry-go-round. This process will continue until the buyer has selected the one that they feel is their Right Door.

Initially, this is the exciting, fun, and easy part of the process. Going in and out of the houses can be fun, interesting, and exciting, similar to riding the merry-go-round. Music is playing, and you're going around and around on the animal of your choice. The ride is easy, predictable, and delightful. The buyer and agent are excited and hopeful that everything will work out for the good in a timely manner. From the seller's perspective, the merry-go-round is typically not as exciting, especially if they reside in their home at the time of the showings. Their safety becomes an issue due to strangers constantly in and out of their houses. It can become very annoying if it goes on for a longer time than expected. Their home is where they tend to have peace, which is challenging to maintain during this time.

Eventually, the buyer finds a house they feel is their home, their "Right Door," and decides to submit an offer. Time to get off the merry-go-round and onto the Ferris wheel. (While on the merry-go-round, the client has not yet entered into an agreement or made any commitments; they have complete control over whether or not they want to continue the ride or get off at any stop. However, the next ride, the Ferris wheel, comes with a little more commitment and less control because more people are involved in the decision-making process).

The Ferris Wheel (Offer)

A Ferris wheel is an amusement ride consisting of a rotating upright wheel with multiple passenger-carrying components (commonly referred to as passenger cars, cabins, tubs, capsules, gondolas, or pods, attached to the rim in such a way that as the wheel turns, they are kept upright usually by gravity). - Wikipedia

The Ferris wheel was designed to be a joyful and delightful ride. At its highest peak, one will feel exhilarated. Similarly, when an offer is accepted, it is one of the happiest and most exhilarating moments in the transaction process, the other being the closing.

Once the client has found what they feel is their Right Door, they will submit an offer; if accepted, they will experience that exhilarating moment. However, if the offer is not accepted, the client will have to get off the ride and go back to the merry-go-round. If they find themselves repeating this cycle too many times, their joy tends to dwindle. If the ride gets stuck at the highest peak (where the client can't immediately walk away), the exhilaration changes to despair and frustration.

For example, a client submits an offer and is waiting and hoping that their offer gets accepted. Sometimes this can take up to several weeks, and they're stuck waiting and hoping for a favorable result. Waiting to get unstuck can be very frustrating, especially if the client feels that they might suffer a loss of some kind if too much time goes by.

Example: The Realtor submits the client's offer; several days pass, and there is no word if the offer had been accepted. The buyer, who has been enjoying their Ferris wheel ride, begins to worry. The ride gets stuck; the buyer is suspended in the air at the top, unsure when and how they will become unstuck. They begin to lose their joy. They want off this ride so that they can continue their journey. As the Realtor, I'm right there beside them, assuring them that they won't be stuck for long and that, eventually, the wheel will begin to spin, and they will get off, with or without an accepted offer. I further assure them that if their offer is not accepted, then there's something better waiting for them, "the right house, at the right price, at the right time."

Typically, during the silent time (when the ride gets stuck), the seller and their agent continue to receive and review other offers, looking for the highest and best. Until there is an accepted offer, the seller is also stuck on this ride.

The next day, the Realtor gets the call that the buyer's offer was not accepted. The Ferris wheel becomes unstuck, and the buyer has a choice to leave the park or stay and get back on the merry-go-round. If the buyer decides to stay, the process can repeat itself several times. Usually, when this happens, these two rides, which were designed to be easy, fun, joyful, and exhilarating, can become annoying and frustrating, and the client begins to lose hope.

After showing several more houses and submitting

several more offers (with no success), the buyer finds another house and submits an offer. Hurray! This time the offer gets accepted. The buyer is thrilled at this point because, to them, this house was better than all the previous houses they had selected. It is now time for the buyer to get off the Ferris wheel and head to the next ride. However, now that there is a binding contract, the next ride is not by choice. (Note: I had clients who only rode the next ride only once and were in and out of the park within thirty days of an accepted offer; however, that is not always the case. Therefore, it's best to carve out some time, pack your patience and be prepared to hang out at the park for a while.)

Note: Once your offer is accepted, DO NOT ESTABLISH ANY NEW CREDIT until after you have closed on your home. Doing this will affect your credit and cause you to either lose your offer on the house or cause a significant delay in your closing (stuck on the Ferris wheel longer than necessary).

The Roller Coaster (Negotiation)

The initial negotiations begin when the offer is submitted (on the Ferris wheel). Those negotiations (if any) are not as daunting because there is no contract involved at that time. It's also not as emotional because the client has not invested much hope, time, or money.

The roller coaster and bumper car rides are where the more daunting and emotional negotiations tend to happen. However, the clients do not ride the bumper car, only the agents. Instead, the clients are affected by the results of the ride. These are the last two rides after a long visit to the park, where everyone is tired and exhausted and wants to get to the closing, exit the park, and get on with their lives.

By this time, both the buyer and seller have invested a lot of time and hope into the process. The buyer is also full of emotions because they also have invested money towards the inspection and appraisal. The home inspection and the real estate appraisal typically are the launching pad for negotiations (unless the buyer waives all contingencies). Boarding the roller coaster ride is where I tell my client to buckle up and hold on tight because the ride could get a bit rocky and turbulent at times.

Roller Coaster - "You can say an experience is a roller coaster, or a roller-coaster ride if it involves many emotional highs and lows, or really good times alternating with really difficult times." - English Club

The buyer and their agent board the roller coaster and buckle their seat belts. The buyer is excited and begins sharing the great news with their family and friends that they have found their Right Door. They begin to imagine how they would furnish and decorate it. The coaster starts to move, and the buyer is excited, looking forward to the first climb. Unfortunately, the inspection report comes back with multiple items reported as deficient, some requiring minor repairs and some major repairs. (This is one of the areas where the term "an emotional roller coaster ride" comes in. If the cost of repairs extends beyond the buyer's budget, their emotions change from excitement to anxiety and concern.)

The thrill of this ride is getting rocky, and the buyer begins to ponder whether they should get off or stay on (in technical terms, submit a mutual release of contract agreement). If they decide to get off the ride, they will either go back on the merry-go-round (begin looking for another home) or leave the park. However, because of the resources already expended and the preparations to relocate, most will choose to stay on and allow their agent to negotiate concessions to satisfy their budget and what they feel is fair. Concessions, typically, would consist of the seller making some or all the repairs or, in some cases, contributing towards the closing cost or lowering the offer price. In some instances, the seller will refuse to give any concessions. If the latter happens, a mutual release of the contract gets executed, and all parties will have to start the process over. However, most sellers will concede to some concession to avoid having to re-start the process. The negotiations can sometimes take a while; therefore, the buyer will continue to experience an emotional roller coaster ride until a mutual agreement is reached.

An appraisal is ordered if there's a mutual agreement with the concessions (sometimes the appraisal is ordered simultaneously with the inspection).

If the appraised value comes in above the offer price, the buyer will have initial equity in the property and, therefore, is happy, and the seller is indifferent. However, if the value is below the offer price, the seller might want the buyer to make up the difference. In most cases, though, the seller will agree to sell at the appraised value because the lender will not lend more than the appraised value. If the buyer has the funds, they might agree to make up the difference in the offer price and the appraised value. This tends to happen in a Seller's Market. A Seller's Market is where there is little inventory and multiple buyers, leading to a bidding war.

The appraisal report is completed and reflects a lesser value than both the listed and offer price. WHOOSH—a fast and rocky drop to the coaster's bottom! This unexpected turn of events leaves the buyer feeling very emotional and anxious, their hope and faith begin to diminish, and they begin to ask, is this really my Right Door? The agent tells them to hold on tight, that they will come out alive, in one piece, no matter how daunting the ride gets. The negotiation begins, the agent submits an amendment for concessions to the seller, based on the inspection and appraisal reports. At this point, the ride is not over. Even though the buyer may be ready to get off, they're stuck until it comes to a complete stop (until the negotiation process is over, and both parties either mutually agree to the amended items or mutually agree to terminate the contract). Several days go by without any response from the other side. After much anxiety, worry, and prayer, the seller's agent finally returns the amendment, signed by the seller, agreeing to lower the offer to the appraised value but only a few concessions towards the repair items—time for the agents to board the bumper car ride.

The Bumper Car (Negotiation)

Bumper Car - Amber Lerner. "Newton's third law of motions comes into play on the bumper cars. This law, the law of interaction, says that if one body exerts a force on a second body, the second body exerts a force equal in magnitude and opposite in direction on the first body. It's the law of action-reaction, and it helps to explain why you feel a jolt when you collide with another bumper car."

(Continuing with the example) The buyer does not have the funds to make any of the repairs, noted by the inspector. This is where the agent gets off the roller coaster and gets into the bumper car. The buyer is still on the roller coaster, and the ride is even more daunting because they have little control, and their fate is in the hands of how well their agent negotiates on their behalf. Therefore, the agent's goal is to negotiate terms that will result in victory for their client. Depending on the disposition of the other agent, this ride can get a bit intrusive.

The optimal goal in negotiating is a win-win outcome; however, that is not always easily accomplished. As agents, our position is to honor our fiduciary duty by negotiating our clients' best deals. And, therefore, the negotiation process may take longer than expected. This is what leads to the bumper car effect. Some agents start every negotiation as if they were going to battle. Their approach can be very annoying to the other agent, and they can find themselves making enemies instead of allies.

This type of agent tends to use negative tactics during the negotiation process. Their approach can also hurt their client's interest, as well, causing them a setback.

One of the tactics used during the negotiation is what I call the bully approach. This tactic occurs when an agent tries to intimidate the other agent into accepting unfair terms for their client. Like the bumper car, the agent unnecessarily, repeatedly, exerts a force. This can show up in many ways, including the agent not agreeing to any concessions. It can also show up in a threatening approach, for instance, a threat to terminate the contract if things don't go their way or threatening to withhold the earnest money deposit (EMD). You can choose to get into that type of bumper car ride or take a strategic approach, making it to the finish line in victory for your client. Ways to achieve this are by being honest, ensuring that your negotiation is ethical and reasonable, knowing policies, documenting all communication, and maintaining all transactions' pertinent documents. Applying this type of approach allows you to maneuver out of the way of unnecessary insults and confrontation and instead allow the other agent to get whiplash by constantly bumping the wall instead of your car. Eventually, they will get exhausted, come to the finish line, and concede to what is right, fair, and just.

Once, I had a client (a seller) who accepted an offer, but the buyer decided not to purchase once the inspection and appraisal reports were completed. My client did not want to release the EMD. He wanted the buyer to suffer a loss to compensate for the time he had lost and, therefore, would not sign the release of the EMD. I told my client that's not how I operate (I don't get on the bumper car ride unnecessarily), that's unethical, and it will not give him back the time he had lost. Therefore, the release was signed, and the EMD returned.

So, when this happened to me, I was furious. If I had to get on this bumper car ride unnecessarily, I was getting on it to win for my client.

There were two instances where I experienced this unnecessary ride and waste of time and energy. The first was with a very intrusive agent. This agent was a seasoned broker (and, therefore, knowledgeable of policies) who knew that her client did not have the right to the EMD. Nevertheless, she tried bullying me with an abrasive approach with her tone and words (very unprofessional). I told her that she could not speak to me in that manner and release the EMD immediately, which she refused. There are several options in settling a situation like this. The two I considered were arbitration and small claims court. Arbitration is expensive but does not take long to get an appointment. Small claims court is less costly but takes too long to get an appointment. Since this was my first experience with this situation, I decided to ask my broker for his suggestion. He suggested that if she did not release the EMD, to go through arbitration. I agreed with him; going through the court system would have taken too long. When I spoke with her again, she was still adamant about not releasing the EMD, so I told her I would see her at arbitration since we could not resolve the issue. After making that statement, she was about to sound off again, so I maneuvered to the finish line and got out of the car (in other words, I hung up on her). I'm sure she was huffing and puffing (bumping her car against the wall getting a whiplash). Her trying to bully me was (actually) ludicrous. Within two days, she released the EMD.

The second time I experienced this unnecessary ride was with an agent who was either ignorant of the policy, naive, or both. Another client of mine decided not to purchase after receiving the inspection report (which consisted of an enormous cost for repairs). Again, due to the lengthy negotiation period and not reaching a mutual agreement, the agent advised their client not to sign the release for the EMD. However, unlike the first agent, this agent (actually) thought their client had the right to the EMD. After several weeks of communication, with no resolution, I finally told her that I would see her at arbitration (this has become my power move when in the bumper car). After that statement, the release was signed and submitted the next day.

Just because the agents felt their clients were entitled to the EMDs, did not give them the right to it; therefore, they, eventually, had to relinquish them. Plus, most agents want to avoid arbitration if they can.

Although this is my least favorite ride in the amusement park, participating in it is unavoidable most times. Therefore, if you ever find yourself on this ride, play fair and by the rules. (There is a saying, "Life is ten percent of what happens to you and ninety percent of what you do about it.") A healthy negotiation is always good, and the ultimate result should be a win-win, but if this doesn't happen, make sure that you apply ethical strategies to end up with the best results for your client. Avoid getting into unnecessary disputes and arguments, but rather, keep a record of all pertinent and required documents. If there is no resolution between the parties, allow the court or intermediaries to resolve any disputes. Applying these strategies is how you win on this ride. Sometimes, you might be dealing with an agent who (actually) loves this ride; therefore, they may want to stay on it unnecessarily, bumping and bumping every chance they can get (in other words, they want to argue rather than negotiate). When this happens, the strategy should be to maneuver to the finish line so that you come off unscathed, leaving the other agent bumping against the wall instead of your car. These two agents were the exception and not the rule. Most agents I have encountered are professional and considerate, with the same goal in mind—getting to the closing.

If the agents find they cannot reach a mutual agreement during negotiations, it's time to walk away from the deal (get off the ride). This situation occurs when neither party is willing to compromise and, therefore, the deal is dead, and a mutual termination agreement is executed. Then, each party goes back to the merry-go-round (buyer finding another house and the seller's listing status goes from pending to back on the market). Fortunately, though, in most cases, the parties usually work out an acceptable deal for each client, realizing that the (ultimate) goal is to get to the closing table.

The roller coaster and bumper car rides can sometimes get very emotional; clients can become frustrated, upset, and even angry. These emotions tend to happen because they are finally near the end of their journey, and after the challenges it took to get to this point, they just want to move on with their lives (they want off these rides). Once I had a client tell me that when they get to closing, they're going to choke the other agent, and another said when they get to the closing, they're not going to speak to the other party. I chuckled and told them that I've never been to a closing where everyone did not have a big smile on their face. The seller gets a check, the buyers get their keys, and at that moment, the power of joy supersedes all the dilemma and drama that took place during the journey. In each of these cases, that's just what happened.

In conclusion (with this example), each party came to a mutual agreement; the seller agreed to make all the repairs. And since both the lender and the title company did not find any other issues, a clear-to-close was issued. So the agent got off the bumper car, and the buyer got off the roller coaster. Everyone went to the closing, grabbed some cotton candy, exited the park, and the client headed to their Right Door.

During the negotiations, I never share the non-pertinent information and nuances of the bumper car experience with my clients. They are already concerned and filled with emotions regarding what the outcome would be and discussing these details will only frustrate them more. Therefore, I only report the outcome and (or) pertinent information (never let your client see you sweat, they have enough on their plate). If my client is someone I know personally, after the closing, I will share some of the behind-the-scene activities that took place so we can have a good laugh.

In life, things tend to get hairy towards the end of a journey; this is because the enemy knows when we are about to walk into our victory, so he attempts to throw obstacles our way to keep us from receiving it. However, if we faint not and keep the faith, we will reap our reward in the end; we will find our Right Door.

The House of Mirrors - Mirror Maze (Disclosure and Code of Ethics)

During my last years as a real estate appraiser, my company ended up on the "blackball list" of a small group of local mortgage companies. The list consisted of appraisers who would not consent to the requests of those mortgage companies that wanted to commit fraud by stretching the values of the properties, which leads to predatory lending. I'm glad I was on that list because the fraud those mortgage companies and banks committed eventually led to over-inflated home values, which inevitably became a huge part of the national market crash of 2008. Being on that list did not affect my business; there was always plenty of work through other upstanding and reputable mortgage companies and banks.

I chose the house of mirrors to symbolize character flaws and the ethical and moral compass. To get an understanding of how the house of mirrors in an amusement park can relate to the Realtor's Code of Ethics is the following descriptions by Wikipedia and Your Dictionary:

House of Mirrors - "A house of mirrors is a traditional attraction at amusement parks. The basic concept behind a house of mirrors is to be a maze-like puzzle. In addition to the maze, participants are also given mirrors as obstacles and glass panes to parts of the maze they cannot yet get to. Sometimes the mirrors may be distorted because of

different curves in the glass to give the participants unusual and confusing reflections of themselves, some humorous and others frightening." - Wikipedia

Hall-of-mirrors (Mirror Maze) – "A confusing and disorienting situation in which it is difficult to distinguish between truth and illusion or between competing versions of reality." - Your Dictionary

Everyone goes through the mirror maze; this is where our reflection is seen. The mirror maze is not a place where you want to hang out too long. Hanging out there too long can cause you to lose sight of yourself, and your illusion can become your reality. However, if we keep our visit here brief, it can be a fun and fascinating experience.

In my youth, the mirror maze was one of my favorite places at the amusement park. I found it fascinating how many ways my reflection became distorted. When I first walked in, I saw my natural reflection. As I continued through the maze, the distortions became comical, reflecting various caricature forms of myself. However, I found that the longer I stayed there and the deeper I went into the maze, the distortions became demonic-looking, and I always knew when it got to that point, it was time to exit. This is what happens if you practice deceiving. Your view of yourself and life can become very complexed and distorted. You will begin to experience variations of your character in a negative view. In real estate, this can happen when a client chooses to be deceptive on their Disclosure Statement.

The Disclosure Statement is a form that the seller fills out. The seller must disclose material defects with the property (material defects are anything that could impact the home's desirability). If the seller is negligent in disclosing the defects, and the buyer becomes affected, the buyer could sue for damages based on fraud. Agents can also be held accountable if they knowingly allow the seller to commit the fraud. Don't be people-pleasers; instead, allow people to reap the benefits of your quest to please God (do the right thing). Deception can also occur in other scenarios, such as the dialog or relationship between agents. This can happen when one or both want to control the contract agreement's outcome above what is honest, fair, and ethical. Although the agent has a fiduciary duty to their client, it does not permit them to be disloyal or unethical to the other party.

Don't be people-pleasers; instead, allow people to reap the benefits of your quest to please God (do the right thing).

According to the National Association of Realtors (NAR)-Code of Ethics and Standards, Article 1 states the following: "When representing a buyer, seller, landlord, tenant, or other parties as an agent, REALTORS® pledge themselves to protect and promote the interests of their client. This obligation to the client is primary, but it does not relieve REALTORS® of their obligation to treat all parties honestly. When serving a buyer, seller, landlord, tenant, or other parties in a non-agency capacity, REALTORS® remain obligated to treat all parties honestly."

Deception is a character flaw that can lead to other negative qualities such as rudeness and dishonesty. Representing yourself in this manner causes your character to become distorted. You might feel like you won, but when it's all said and done, you've (actually) lost; you have lost your soul. In the quest to deceive the other party, you have deceived yourself. You have just assisted your client in entering or exiting the Wrong Door. As stated in the NAR Code of Ethics, agents are obligated to treat all parties honestly. From my experience, I'm glad to say that most agents that I have encountered adhere to the Realtors' Code of Ethics & Standards of Practice described by the National Realtors Association and referenced at the end of this book.

When I was blackballed, I'm glad that I did not succumb to those mortgage lenders' requests. Because when the great market crash of 2008 happened, those appraisers and mortgage lenders who committed or were complicit in the fraud found themselves either in jail, having their license provoked, having to pay fines, or all the above. The proverbial saying **"man's rejection is God's protection"** is so true.

Earlier, I mentioned that we should all discover our strengths and weaknesses, as they relate to our personality and character and how important they are in the way we show up to others. The mirror maze is an excellent place to discover what they are. When we look at our physical reflection in the glass mirror, we see what others see when they look at us. The same applies when we look inside ourselves, the essence of who we are. Others see that as well, not with their eyes, but how they feel when they are in your presence. People are our reflections; they respond to us through reciprocity. Therefore, it is essential to be honest with ourselves and not deny our flaws (weaknesses). They are not going away unless we do the work.

When we look in the glass mirror and see a rash or pimple on our face, we immediately try to find solutions to eliminate or minimize it. Similarly, we must find ways to eliminate or at least mitigate our internal flaws. Even if we choose not to see or accept those undesirable traits, others can still see them. They see them through our conduct, actions, and words, and they sense our energy. The great poet Maya Angelou once said, "I've learned that people will forget what you said, people will forget what you did, but people will never forget how you made them feel."

We may be able to temporarily fake it, but our true selves will eventually surface. Just like applying a Band-Aid to cover that rash on our face will not cause it to go away, it is the same with our inner flaws—applying a Band-Aid will not cause them to disappear. Instead, we must do the work to eliminate them so we will not have to worry about being exposed when the Band-Aid falls off.

Another area agents should be mindful and respectful of is the differences in others. This includes race, culture, ethnicity, sexual orientation, religion, etc. We should never assume that everyone is on the same page as us. To do this would require, mindfully, giving respect to another's requests or wishes regarding their boundaries, even when we think it is not necessary or essential. Following is an example of what I experienced with another agent:

An agent contacted me to make an offer for one of my listings. I noticed in his email the following: "I am not available after 5:00 pm on Friday through Sunday morning; this is my family time". I assumed that statement was religion-related (but it should be respected regardless, even if it wasn't). Therefore, out of common courtesy, I made sure that I never attempted to contact him during that time, even though there were times that I needed an immediate response to an issue.

Weeks later, after the closing, the agent came to pick up the keys from my client's house; it was our first meeting in person. Upon our greeting, he thanked me and told me that it was nice working with me, and when we concluded the key exchange, he headed toward his car to leave. Then, suddenly, he turned around and came back to where my client and I were standing. When he approached us, he said to my client, "You have a very professional and kind agent; this is not always the case, and if ever you have any referrals, you should refer them to her." He was my reflector that day.

In conclusion, you don't want to hang out in the mirror maze too long, entertaining distorted, demonic versions of yourself; instead, do the work and allow the best you to show up. Never lose focus of who you are or present yourself in a negative, deceitful, or distorted way, where you may have to ask yourself,

"Mirror, mirror, on the wall, who am I?"

FINDING THE RIGHT DOOR

Finding the Right Door is imperative for your peace of mind. Your Right Door is the place where you should be, and when you are, you'll experience peace in your life. Because we are all uniquely different, knowing who you are is imperative when finding your Right Door. Comparing, coveting, or measuring yourselves to others, will inevitably affect your peace. Your home should reflect your taste and personality.

I have seen many different styles and designs of houses during my years of appraising. What I noticed and what stood out to me the most were the homes that reflected the homeowner's personality. There was a house on the northwest side of Detroit; it was a smaller house, approximately 900 square feet. From the time I stepped inside, I was in awe. The interesting artifacts, and the meticulous arrangement of the furniture and accessories, were awe-inspiring. My experience there was more than what I saw, but also how I felt. In our conversation, I discovered that he was a creative artist; his decor reflected his personality. Several weeks later, I appraised a house for a couple located in Bloomfield Hills (a suburb). This house was approximately 3800 square feet. I remembered experiencing the same level of awe as the smaller home in Detroit. It was impeccably furnished and designed, which reflected the personalities of the homeowners.

We all can get ideas and inspiration from others

(especially those who have similar tastes as ours); it's when we try to fit into someone else's mold that can cause us to lose ourselves, get off our paths, and make it difficult to find our Right Door. As the saying goes, "it's better to be one hundred percent of who you are than fifty percent of someone else." Therefore, it's imperative to allow God to direct our paths so we can stay on the one He has planned for us.

Also, once you have found your Right Door, never let anyone else's opinion persuade you or talk you out of it. I have seen family members and friends of some of my clients give the side-eye and a raised eyebrow because they didn't like the house that the client had chosen. I also heard comments such as, *"the house is too small or too large," or they didn't like this or that.* Number one, they are not going to live there, you are; and number two, they're certainly not going to pay your mortgage. They are looking from the natural eye and their taste. They cannot experience what you felt and acknowledged from within when you walked into your Right Door, and it's something you can't fully explain (even if you tried, they wouldn't fully understand) because it's your experience.

Finally, avoid settling when searching for your Right Door. Settling will cause you to end up with the wrong door. I have witnessed a few of my clients who came close to becoming homeless and, therefore, began to panic. Because of this, they ask me to find something opposite from their criteria; they were willing to settle for the wrong door. I'm glad to say that they found their Right Door before they had to settle.

Another situation involved a friend of mine, whose lease on her apartment was about to expire, and instead of renewing the lease, she decided to purchase a home. Although she was not my client, she asked if she could consult with me throughout the process. Therefore, I suggested that she request a month-to-month on her lease so that she would not feel pressed or have to settle when finding her new home and pray that everything would work out in the end. She got approved for the month-to-month, and after many months of searching, she finally found a house, submitted an offer, and was approved. However, after several weeks of non-communication with her lender, she finally contacted them and discovered that she was never approved for the loan. The pre-approval letter was not legitimate, and, therefore, she did not get the house. After talking with her about the situation, I found out that she did not even like the house; she was settling because she felt pressed. I told her that it was a blessing that she was not approved for that loan because she would have entered the Wrong Door and had no peace. A month later, she was approved with another lender and, shortly after that, found and closed on her Right Door.

Next, I will take you on a journey through the amusement park when finding my Right Door, and with the experiences of seven of my clients in their pursuit of finding their Right Door. The lessons that I learned throughout the journeys and experiences as a Realtor has increased my faith level. *You never know the level of your faith until you are tested.* Hebrews 11:6 says, "Without faith, it is impossible to please God." In the same way, without faith, it is impossible to get to closing without much worry and anxiety. Finding the Right Door can at times be a very daunting and even arduous journey, especially amid other life issues. Therefore, it is imperative to have some level of faith when going through this process.

My Right Door

My trip to the amusement park was short; I rode each ride only once. At the time I was looking for my home, I was a licensed real estate appraiser and had a pretty good idea of what I was looking for in a home. Having gone inside many houses, I was familiar with the areas and neighborhoods that I was interested in; therefore, my ride on the merry-go-round was short because I chose not to view many of the houses my agent presented me. To help narrow my search, I made a list of the amenities I was looking for and my must-haves.

I looked at a few houses that included some of the amenities on my list throughout my search, but when I first stepped inside, I knew they were not my Right Door; I did not feel a sense of peace. I continued to search, and within thirty days, I found my house and was off the merry-go-round and onto the Ferris wheel. That ride was short also, one time around without incident. I presented an offer lower than the asking price; the seller countered my offer; I stood firm on my initial offer, and the seller conceded (all within a few hours).

I also rode the roller coaster only once. The ride was exhilarating and not daunting at all. This was because there were no negotiations. The appraisal came in above my offer price, and I did not have a home inspection. However, I did not escape this experience unscathed; my dilemma came after the closing. My agent acted as a dual agent (an agent to both the seller and me).

Because of that dual agency relationship, I experienced a house of mirrors situation regarding an obvious omission in the seller's disclosure. I discovered the issue on the first day I moved in. It was partly my fault because I failed to get a home inspection. **(WARNING: NEVER, EVER NOT GET A HOME INSPECTION.)**

When I found my Right Door, it did not have some of the amenities that were on my list; it also needed many updates. I must mention again, "The Right Door" does not mean the "Perfect Door." Why did I purchase a property that did not include some of the amenities on my list and needed updating? I bought it because it was my Right Door at that time. When I stepped into my house for the first time, I felt a sense of peace; I felt at home. It was that intangible feeling that God was speaking to me via the Holy Spirit. Although it did not have some of the amenities on my list, it did have two of my essential "must-haves." 1) neighborhood security and 2) layout, or as the Chinese would say, "feng shui," which means that the layout or floor plan brings a certain energy into the room. I did not know much about this saying then and, therefore, did not base my feelings or intuition on it. But, from my experience, there must be some truth to it, because, as I mentioned earlier, I looked at several houses that had most of the amenities that were on my list, but because of the layout and lack of sunlight, I did not have a sense of comfort or peace. The safety issue was also significant to me. I'm glad I trusted my instincts because, after many years, I still have a sense of security; and amenities can always be added, but it is more costly to change a layout.

Further confirmation that this was my Right Door came years later when I tried to walk away from my home. At that time, my house went into foreclosure (no fault of my own) because of an error made by the bank (which, later, I benefitted from through several class-action lawsuits). After endlessly trying to resolve the bank issue, I finally got fed up and decided to walk away from my home and start over elsewhere. I tried walking through other doors to no avail and was quickly becoming homeless. Finally, I decided to be still, get quiet and pray, and within two weeks, the situation was resolved. I reclaimed my house for a nominal price, the entire previous mortgage loan balance was erased, and I walked back through my Right Door.

It is vitally important to listen to the Holy Spirit (or that gut feeling), be obedient, and, by faith, trust in God and allow Him to guide and direct our paths. I do not always do this, but I'm glad I did this time. Because God knows the beginning and the end, He knew that another turn of events in my life was about to occur, and because of this, I believe He did not want me to enter the Wrong Door by leaving my Right Door. Had I not been obedient and entered the Wrong Door (purchased another property or rented a high-priced apartment), my financial peace would have been disturbed. I would have been without a healthy peace of mind, and because of that, it would have been difficult to carry out my assignments (I find it difficult to serve others wholeheartedly when I'm not at peace in my own life).

God knew what was ahead (I didn't have a clue), and I

am glad that I chose to be obedient because one year later, after reclaiming my home, I was hit with a financial loss when the City of Detroit declared bankruptcy. As a retiree, my pension was reduced, and I lost my health benefits. I saw none of this coming, but God did. Because He's my protector, He kept me hidden until He worked things out.

Again, how do I know my home was the Right Door? I know because of the peace I have in my life. It's because of that peace that God can use me for the purpose He has planned for me through my assignments. In finding the Right Door, we might have to compromise on some amenities, but we should never have to compromise on our peace. I wonder if I had gotten an inspection and known about the repairs before closing, would I have purchased this house? I believe that God does not reveal everything to us (at once) because it might cause us to make different decisions and choose different paths than those He wants us to take. Because we do not know what the future will bring, by faith, trusting in God is key (Proverbs 3:5,6).

Prelude – Clients Story

Realtors wear many hats and play many different roles when assisting their clients. As a Realtor, I have played the role of counselor, minister, attorney, accountant, and prayer warrior. Most of my clients are family, friends, and referrals from them. I found that working with people with whom I have a close relationship has its pros and cons. Sometimes, it is not easy because I experience each ride alongside them and can sense their emotions. On the pro side, it is rewarding that I get the opportunity to help and assist them in one of their most significant life-changing decisions, which, sometimes, coincides with other stressful and challenging dilemmas in their lives.

I have had clients who were not experiencing any other life dilemma or drama, nor did any arise during the process with the other client and agent. The day at the amusement park was fun and delightful, having to ride each ride only once and some not at all; thereby, having more time to enjoy other park activities. However, that is rarely the case; most people looking to relocate are simultaneously experiencing other dilemmas. Therefore, I chose seven of my clients to tell their stories. Each one was, simultaneously, experiencing different life's challenges and dilemmas while on their journey of finding their Right Door. Because of my close relationship with most of them, I rode each ride alongside them. The day at the park was long, exciting, adventurous, thrilling, and daunting. Along with our picnic baskets, we also had to pack our survival kits, filled with faith and patience.

Let's get into the stories of these seven clients and their journeys in finding their Right Door. For privacy purpose, I will refer to them as Client I, Client II, Client III, Client IV, Client V, Client VI, and Client VII .

Client I - The Mice

One of my biggest fears and only phobia is anything in the rodent family; there's something about those creatures that make my flesh crawl! Client I is someone near and dear to me, so when she contacted me about selling her house and finding a new one, of course, I said yes, I would be honored. When selling and buying a home simultaneously, the agent and client may have to ride the same rides more than once and sometimes simultaneously. Also, there is always the possibility that the client could temporarily become homeless. As agents, this is one of our greatest challenges, making sure that our client transfers from one house to the next in a timely manner. Therefore, the strategies that we implement must work out timely. One of those strategies is applying contingencies to the contract. In this case, we included a 30-day occupancy contingency in the contract. The 30-day occupancy allows the seller to occupy the premises up to 30 days after the closing for an agreed upon occupancy fee. We could have requested more days but felt confident the additional 30 days after closing would be enough time to find and close on the new house. Also, requesting too many days can potentially drive buyers away because most buyers want to move in as soon as possible.

Immediately after listing the property, we received several requests for showings. The problem was that the potential buyers did not qualify for the asking price. This merry-go-round ride went on for a while before Client I decided to do some minor touch-ups on her home. Therefore, we agreed to place a conditional withdrawal on the listing. In the meantime, we continued to search for her new home.

Client I had selected two areas where she was interested in buying. After several weeks of searching and finding no listings that met her criteria, we ventured out to other areas. However, even after including other areas, we continued to be stuck on the merry-go-round. The reason for this was because it was a seller's market, and the inventory was low. On the contrary, we relisted her property during this same time, and within the first week, we received an offer, which the seller accepted.

Time was now of the essence; we had to find her new home and close on it before homeless status ensued. After several weeks of searching, Client I found a house and submitted an offer. It was not in the area she had hoped for, but she decided to compromise since it possessed most of her criteria. So, off the merry-go-round, onto the Ferris wheel. The offer was accepted, and the home inspection was scheduled.

Typically, both the client and agent will meet with the inspector at the property, but Client I decided not to come out that day. Therefore, only I met with the inspector at the house. As we walked through the house, the inspector pointed out the defects. I began to feel a little depressed, not only because of what he was revealing but also, the house did not look the same as it did the first time Client I and I were there. Our first visit was during extenuating circumstances. Before viewing this house, we had viewed many others and even submitted offers to a few that were not accepted; she now had only a little more than thirty days before moving out of her existing home. Therefore, pressed for time, when we walked through the house, we were more focused on the criteria and amenities on her "must-haves" list, which the house contained most of; therefore, we felt this was the one. However, the inspector pointed out many defects that Client I and I did not notice during our initial walk-through. Especially, the baited mouse traps throughout the house. As I stated earlier, always get a home inspection!

I decided to wait in the living room while the inspector completed the report on his laptop. As he was about to print out the report, the inspector remembered that he forgot to inspect the attic. Therefore, he pulled out his ladder and proceeded to check the attic. As I was sitting there, waiting on him to conclude his inspection, looking around that room and thinking about all the defects and mouse traps, I got an eerie feeling; something was amiss. I felt that my client was not going to be happy there. I began thinking about how I could convince her to walk away and continue looking, even though we were pressed for time. I knew it would be difficult because the buyers for her house were closing the next week, which would leave my client thirty days from the closing date to find and close on her new home. As I was thinking about all that, I heard the inspector say, "OH NO! this doesn't look good." He stated that there were mice droppings and holes in the insulation where the mice had eaten it. He also said that the pest control company probably had not discovered how the mice were getting in, which explains why the containers (of a reputable pest control company) were situated throughout the house. Well, that's all I needed to hear on top of everything else I was already feeling. The evidence of mice is one thing, but the fact that a professional company has not discovered how they were getting in is even a bigger problem. For me, that would be a deal-breaker. As I explained earlier, the Right Door is a place where you should have peace, and not knowing how or to what extent it would take to get rid of the rodents would (definitely) affect my peace. However, though, I'm not the one purchasing the property. Therefore, I wasn't sure if this would be a deal-breaker for my client.

After the inspection was completed, I contacted Client I to report everything in the inspector's report, including the mice. I mentioned that I was not getting good vibes about the place, but ultimately, it was her decision. I did not have to convince her, though, because, as soon as I mentioned the mice situation, she immediately said: "I'm Out!" Therefore, I submitted a mutual release, and we continued our search. Back on the merry-go-round!

The day of the closing for her existing property had come, and for the first time, Client I began to worry and became concerned about the reality that she could become homeless. Time was of the essence! We now had less than thirty days to find and close on her new home. To prevent Client I from becoming homeless, we even began looking at leases as a temporary solution. There was one lease that she decided to settle for and asked me to put in an application. After approximately a week had gone by with no word from the leasing agent, I decided to call and leave a message. A few more days passed, and I still had not heard from the leasing agent; therefore, I told my client that he must have gone with another applicant. We were now searching relentlessly, going in and out of leases and sales. This merry-go-round ride was no longer as joyful, hopeful, or fun; we both were ready to get off but knew it was not an option, so we continued to ride. We now had approximately twenty-five days left before she would have to vacate the premises of her existing home. We continued to keep our faith, hope, and spirits up. We never spoke doubtful words even though, as each day passed, it drew her closer to becoming homeless.

But God! a listing hit the market, located in her number one chosen area. We wasted no time scheduling a showing which we were approved for the following day. After the showing, we immediately submitted an offer. Off the merry-go-round and onto the Ferris wheel. Because I knew that there would be a high demand due to the low inventory, I could not let this one get away. Therefore, I called the agent to see if she had received other offers before submitting the offer. She informed me that she had three so far and that two were at the asking price and one above. I considered the information as I prepared the offer.

After discussing the situation with Client I, we submitted the offer, and after two days, it was approved. I thought this was great; we will close before she would become homeless. But then the Ferris wheel became stuck! What's going on? What was causing the delay? I knew something was not right because, by now, we should have had a clear-to-close. When I did not hear from my Client I, I gave her a call; she informed me that she had opened an account at a hardware store to receive a discount on a particular item. She stated that she thought her credit would not be affected because she made a very minimum purchase (less than $100). As the agent, I felt bad because I did not warn her of this. I was also disappointed with the financial agent because the financial agent is responsible for informing the client of all financial matters regarding the loan approval. Typically, the lender will give the client a list of dos and don'ts when applying for a mortgage loan. Fortunately, this matter got resolved within two days, and we got a clear-to-close. Off the Ferris wheel onto the roller coaster.

We only had to ride the roller coaster once, which was great because, by this time, she had less than three weeks left to close on the new house and move out of the existing home. After the inspection, we submitted an amendment for repairs, which was approved.

The closing took place with five days left to move out of her existing property. Not only did she make the deadline, but she also left her existing property impeccably clean, with a day to spare. The day I met with the buyers to exchange the keys, they expressed how grateful they were to have found their dream home and how pleased they were with how impeccable the seller had left it. Although Client I was pressed for time, because of her integrity, she considered the buyer's well-being. Although there were many hurdles and pressures for time, it all worked out in the end. Client I walked into her Right Door, at the right time and for the right price.

Sometimes, being pressed for time can cause one to settle for something other than their Right Door. This was the case with two previous offers submitted by Client I that were not accepted (man's rejection is God's protection). Oh, by the way, the leased property, where I never heard from the landlord, I found out later (after searching through my paperwork) that I never even submitted the application. I found that interesting because I had never done that before.

While mice might not be a deal-breaker for you, whatever your deal-breaker is, don't ignore it. I have heard stories of people settling, out of pressure or fear of becoming homeless, only to find themselves miserable because they ended up somewhere where they had no peace. In this case, the house was located in a nice suburban neighborhood. It also contained most of the criteria and "must-haves" Client I was looking for. However, the mice situation was a deal-breaker and, therefore, was not her Right Door. I also found the mice situation disturbing because it was not disclosed on the Sellers Disclosure Form. I mentioned it to the listing agent, who stated she was unaware of it. I found that odd because the pest control boxes were visible. This is an example of the mirror house, which negatively affects the integrity of the Agent.

Note: Once you have been approved for a mortgage loan, do not do anything life-changing, such as quit your job or take out new credit loans until after you have closed. Your credit is monitored up to the date of closing. It does not matter how small or large the line of credit is. Hits to your credit score and changes to your debt-to-income ratio set off alarms with lenders, which affects your loan qualification, which can cause you to lose out on your home or delay the process.

Client II - The NACA Program

The Neighborhood Assistance Corporation of America (NACA) Program is a great program designed to assist many people across the country to become homeowners. The program enables some borrowers to purchase a home with little or no down payment or closing costs. The NACA Program makes homeownership more attainable for more people, especially people with limited funds and/or credit profiles. The program is a non-profit community homeownership advocacy organization. NACA is not a lender but works with participating lenders to offer the program to home buyers.

There are two classifications of people who qualify for this program. 1) The priority members: those considered low-to-moderate-income households, and 2) The non-priority members: those whose income exceeds the low-to-moderate income but whose credit may not qualify them with mainstream lenders. The priority members are qualified for up to one hundred percent of the down payment and closing costs but are limited to where they can purchase. The non-priority members may be eligible for some assistance towards the down payment and closing costs (depending on their income), and there are no limits to where they can purchase. As of 2017, the non-priority members' purchase must not have exceeded $484,350 (this figure is subject to change throughout the years). Both groups must complete the required home-buyer workshops to be considered eligible to participate in the program. Client II was in the non-priority group and therefore was not limited to any specific areas. They were able to choose a home in any participating area within their state.

Although this is a great program, I must warn you that you might find yourself at the amusement park all day, so pack your patience, get prayed up, release your faith, and know that if you faint not, it will all work out in the end. This program requires a lot of time and patience; therefore, I praise God for giving me the wisdom to work on this area in my life, which made me better prepared for this assignment when it came along.

From my experience, this program required more time to get qualified and clear-to-close than any other program, including FHA. These delays tend to happen with non-profit organizations due to the red tape involved in the process. This program was a learning experience for both my clients and me.

Client II is a husband-and-wife team whom I have a close and personable relationship with. In my initial meeting with Client II, they informed me that their lease would expire soon, and they wanted to purchase a home. They explained that in addition to their criteria and amenities, they also had two must-haves. For her, it was the dining area because she knew soon that she would take over hosting Thanksgiving dinners for the family in honor of her mother. And for him, the man cave must have a particular layout for his music studio and entertainment area.

Client II had more than the required funds, but their credit needed some improvement. Therefore, they decided to qualify through the NACA Program. In the beginning, it seemed like a fantastic program. Anytime Client II had questions, they were able to contact their case manager and got an immediate response. However, once they began the workshops and counseling classes, things began to change. There were long delays with getting signed up from one class to another, and the communication with the case manager became distant, making it difficult for them to complete their classes and get approved for the loan. This lapse in communication caused them to worry because time was running out on their existing lease. The classes were designed to be completed within a specific time; however, it took them longer than the required time due to the case manager's lack of communication. Despite the delays, they persevered and finally completed the required classes and got their approval. Off to the amusement park!

First stop, the merry-go-round! Everyone was happy and excited about the possibilities. For approximately four months, they looked at many houses and submitted several offers. This process involved going from the merry-go-round to the Ferris wheel and back again. Each time their offer got rejected, they became more and more frustrated, and the stress was mounting. Although they submitted offers equivalent to the asking price and sometimes above, they continued to get outbid. I explained that we were in a "sellers' market," which tends to cause a bidding war. Bidding wars tend to happen when there is low inventory which causes many buyers to compete for the same property, overbidding the asking price (which inevitably drives up the market value). Bidding wars are challenging for buyers but great for sellers, as sellers are in a position to choose between multiple offers typically above the asking price.

The dilemma with the NACA Program is that the client has a specific amount of time to find and close on a property before the specified program deadline. If they do not meet the deadline, they will have to start part, or all, of the process over, depending on the length of the delay. Client II found themselves in that situation. As they continued to search for their home, one of the steps in the process had expired, and therefore, they had to submit more paperwork before continuing. During this same time, they were experiencing personal difficulty. Her beloved mother's health was declining, and one of the things Client II had hoped for was that her mother would get to see her new home before her passing. Needless to say, the merry-go-round ride had become not so merry; trying to ride with a heavy heart is difficult. Because I knew and loved her mother also, it was a solemn time for us all. With this happening and the program delays, things became frustrating and annoying at times for my clients while trying to meet the deadlines. Through it all, though, they managed to keep their spirits up. He was always there to support her, and she pressed through with dignity and grace as they continued the ride, searching for their Right Door. (We even took some time between the merry-go-round and Ferris wheel rides to stop and get some refreshments.)

Finally (with only a month to go before another program step would expire), they found another house. They liked this house better than all the previous ones. This one had the must-haves that they each were looking for and more. Because they really wanted this house, I reminded them of the bidding war, and therefore be prepared to make a winning offer. In the meantime, I contacted the listing agent to inquire if there had been other offers. She informed me that she had received multiple offers, most over the asking price and that she would accept the highest and best before six that evening. I knew I would not have the offer in by that time; therefore, I asked if she could hold off on her decision until I had submitted my client's offer. She agreed. After consulting with my clients, they submitted an accepted offer. They felt this was their Right Door and did not want to lose out on it. The seller was pleased with the offer, but the agent was reluctant about the NACA Program because she had never heard of it. Since I was informed and believed (at that time) it was great program and that the process of getting a clear-to-close was even more efficient than some of the other popular programs, I was able to convince her of this too. They accepted the offer, and we were finally able to get off the merry-go-round (for the last time) and onto the Ferris wheel.

Well, contrary to what I was told and believed, our experience with the NACA Program was not that great when it came to a timely closing. Once an offer gets accepted in a typical transaction, the only other entities involved are the lender and title company. However, with the NACA Program, the case manager is an intermediate party in the process, and therefore, everything moves at a slower pace (red tape). That, along with the lack of communication, really slowed things down, resulting in frustration for us all. We were stuck on the Ferris wheel much too long. With the NACA Program, there is a process when submitting an offer that requires several documents that the clients and their agents must complete. You cannot proceed to the next step unless the case manager approves the documents. Because of this process, I got frustrated when my clients or I could not contact the case manager. After several voice messages and emails with no response, I contacted someone at headquarters to explain the situation. That got the ball rolling, but unfortunately, we had passed another deadline by this time, and the buyers had to re-submit updated documents again.

Once the documents were submitted and approved, we were off the Ferris wheel and onto the roller coaster. The second hurdle came with the inspection process. The program's policy requires that only inspectors approved by the program can perform the inspection. Also, all repairs noted by the inspector must be completed at the seller's expense, then a re-inspection is ordered by the buyer. Well, because the seller decided to make all the repairs himself, instead of hiring a professional, it took three re-inspections and approximately three weeks before we eventually received a clear-to-close. By far, due to the numerous re-inspections, this was the longest roller coaster ride I had experienced. I had to get off the ride several times to go for my fitness-therapy-meditation walks. And as always, I came back refreshed, charged up, and ready to finish out the ride with positive energy and clearer thoughts. The trade-off from the long ride on the roller coaster was that there were no further negotiations, and I did not have to get on the bumper car ride. In conclusion, as I stated earlier, this is a great program if all parties involved do their due diligence on all that is required, especially with communication.

Although Client II experienced more delays than necessary, their journey was very interesting. We all learned a lot about the NACA Program, and it all worked out in the end—they found their Right Door. She continues to host annual Thanksgiving Dinners for her family; he continues to live out his passion, creating music in his state-of-the-art studio. In addition, they enjoy entertaining their friends and family in their outstanding movie studio, entertaining area. Unfortunately, though, her mother never got the chance to see their beautiful home in person. However, Client II stated that her mother's spirit is there, especially during Thanksgiving dinners.

Client III - The Relocation

Client III is a husband and wife whom I have known for many years. One day they contacted me to tell me that they were planning on moving and would like me to list their property (where they had resided for over forty years). They stated that they had not decided whether to purchase their new home in Michigan or relocate out of state. I told them, sure, I'll be happy to, and thanks for choosing me as their Realtor. The day I met with them to complete the paperwork, they informed me that they had decided to relocate out of state. I found this amazing since they were both in their seventies. It goes to show that life is to continue to be enjoyed and lived till the end. They also stated that they were going to purchase rather than rent. Therefore, the sale of their home had to be in sync with their new home's purchase. They further stated that they chose me because they knew I could get it done. I had to ask myself, was I up for the challenge? I did not necessarily need the money—was this worth the stress and jeopardizing a friendship if things didn't work out according to their plans? I decided to take on the challenge (binding the fear of failure that entered my thoughts, and instead, chose to operate out of faith that it would all work out).

Onto the merry-go-round! Fortunately, this was a short ride; within two days of listing the property, we had an offer for the asking price. Onto the Ferris wheel! Because Client III was still residing in their home at the time, they were happy to receive an acceptable offer so soon because it meant that they did not have to experience a lot of traffic in and out of their home. Therefore, they accepted the offer immediately. Off the Ferris wheel and onto the roller coaster! The inspection and appraisal reports came back with only a few minor items that needed repairs that the seller could make himself. Ok, I'm thinking, this is great, this is going to be easy, one of the fastest deals I've had. I even told my clients that they should be thinking of a Plan B because they probably would be closing on their existing home before finding their new home. But just when we thought everything was moving right along, everything on the other end got very quiet; there was a long silent period.

I left several messages with the buyer's agent, with no response. During this period, communication is essential because now a contract is active, more people and entities are involved, and everyone needs to be on the same page. Also, time is of the essence. Typically, negotiations can spark a range of emotions, which can be frightening and daunting, similar to a roller coaster with its steep inclines and speedy plunges. During the silent times, those emotions are heightened. That is due to the unknown; not knowing why you are stuck on the ride could lead to anxiety and fear. During the silent time, the ride becomes very daunting—not only are you stuck, but you're also in darkness. You cannot see what is coming next. The feeling is eerie because you do not know how long you will be stuck or what the result will be when you become unstuck. As for my clients, they wondered if they should postpone their plans to relocate.

Client III were calling me, and I did not have specific answers for them regarding the silence. I explained to them that, typically, the other agent is working things out with their client during the quiet time, and it probably had something to do with their finances. However, since I still had not spoken with the other agent, I was unsure if that was the case. During the quiet time, the mystery of the unknown is where faith and prayer come in. My clients asked me to please pray over the situation, which I did. In the meantime, they decided to continue with their plans and had flown to the other state several times, searching and bidding on properties. As each day came and went, my clients became more anxious and disheartened with no word from the buyer's side; they felt they had no control over the situation. One time, after getting back from the other state, Client III decided she would not allow her hope and faith to be diminished. She told me that she had prayed over the situation. She felt she could do nothing else at this point, so instead of being stuck on the roller coaster (in other words, sitting and worrying about the situation), she asked if I could meet her for a walk. So, we got off the roller coaster, went walking, and got some cotton candy.

It was now going on two weeks since being stuck on the roller coaster. I now had to leave a different type of message (I had to leave my clients on the roller coaster and get on the bumper car). I must keep this ball rolling for the sake of my clients. If the buyer does not qualify, I need to know (immediately) so that I can relist the property. After getting that last message from me, the agent finally called back. He informed me that the buyers did not have all their closing costs and depended on a family member to help them out. But the family member was reluctant because she did not feel comfortable disclosing her financial information with the lender. At least, we now knew what the hold-up was all about. Knowing this information shed some light, lessened the mystery, and, in turn, allowed us to make an informed decision.

After that conversation, I decided that I would submit a mutual release and start the process over. Needless to say, my clients were very disappointed that they had wasted so much time with that buyer. I reluctantly prepared the mutual release but did not send it right away. Instead, I prayed for a favorable outcome. I did not want my clients starting over, having people traipsing through their house again. Two days later, the buyer's agent contacted me to say that the family member contacted her attorney, who helped her understand that her financial information would be safe and secure. The next day, he called to tell me that she now felt safe sharing her financial information. That was great news; we were able to proceed toward the closing.

Finally, the buyers got approved for their mortgage loan and a clear-to-close. So, we were able to get off the roller coaster and close on the property timely. That day at the park was filled with excitement and thrills, which we were all too glad to exit.

Although we did not have to negotiate any concessions, the roller coaster ride caused my clients to be filled with dismay due to the mystery (the quiet time). During that time, one might feel vulnerable and have no control over the situation, which tends to cause anxiety. However, no matter the situation or predicament, there is always an escape. There are always choices—they might not be convenient, but they are available. In this case, if the buyer was not able to secure their finances, we would have submitted a mutual release and started the process over.

What's amazing is that Client III found and closed on their new house (in the other state) within two weeks from closing on their existing home. And because they had a 30-day occupancy contingency, they were able to transfer from what was once their Right Door to their new Right Door without becoming homeless. It all worked out in the end; they are now enjoying their new home and living their best lives. Also, I am happy to report that our friendship is still intact, and I plan to visit them in their new home someday soon.

Client IV - The Divorce

This case was one of my most interesting and complex. I received a phone call from the husband, who stated that they were selling their home and buying a new one, and they wanted me to be their Realtor. No problem, I got this. Well, so I thought! After about two weeks of meeting with the clients, listing the property, and sending them listings for their new home, I got a phone call stating they were getting a divorce. Hold up! Stop the ride! Are you kidding me!

On top of that, they both wanted me to represent them as their buyer's agent for their new homes. Initially, I was not going to represent the husband. However, the wife, who is near and dear to me, stated she had no problem with me representing him. I reluctantly acquiesced. (By the way, I do not recommend this). Time to head to the amusement park.

Typically, I look forward to going to the amusement park, but not this time. Due to the circumstances, I felt it was more like going to combat rather than an adventure. I had to do what Apostle Paul said in Ephesians 6:11; "put on the whole armour of God." Also, I had hoped that we would not have to enter the house of mirrors by either party confiding in me the reason for the divorce. That would have (definitely) made things more awkward.

Because I was operating as both the seller's and buyer's agent, we had to ride each ride simultaneously and some multiple times. Fortunately, though, selling their home did not require much drama and time. The merry-go-round ride lasted approximately a week before we had received an offer and was on the Ferris wheel. After that, the other rides went rather quickly. Typically, this is a listing agent's dream, but it was quickly becoming a nightmare in this case. After closing on their property, and due to the thirty-day occupancy agreement, they had to find and close on their new homes before becoming homeless.

Finding their new homes was not as expeditious as selling their home. Typically, the merry-go-round is full of joy and happiness (hence the word "merry"), but not in this case. That was the bumpiest merry-go-round ride I've ever experienced, and we had not even made it to the other rides yet. I always go over and beyond for my clients. This case was no exception.

Since they both had the same criteria and even chose some of the same areas, they received some of the same listings. I hoped and prayed that they would not end up choosing the same listing. Well, that prayer was not answered; they both decided that they wanted this particular house. I had shown it to him first. Although it was a little above his price range, he wanted to make an offer anyway. Because he decided to continue to look at other properties, he delayed submitting an offer. In the meantime, the wife wanted to view the same property. I informed her that he was interested in that one and was thinking about submitting an offer. Since he had not submitted his offer yet, she insisted on viewing the property. Well, of course, she also liked it, and even though it was also out of her chosen price range, she still considered submitting an offer.

A few days later, the husband called to tell me that he was ready to make an offer on the house. I informed the wife of this, and after a few hilarious and other words, she said that she had no problem with him making the offer. Whoosh! Off the merry-go-round and onto the Ferris wheel. This is when I am simultaneously riding the Ferris wheel with him and the merry-go-round with her. The ride on the Ferris wheel did not last long because his offer was not accepted, back on the merry-go-round with him. We all are still riding this ride looking for houses, and time is running out. My greatest concern was that I did not want them to become homeless, especially her.

A week later, he found a house he liked, and his offer was accepted. We rode the other rides without incident. Finally, he closed on his new home and left the park. In the meantime, the wife was still stuck on the merry-go-round. Even though she was going through one of the most difficult times in her life, she kept her spirits up. My assignment was to be there for her, to assist her in finding her Right Door. That was one of the times I did not aggravate about riding the merry-go-round more than necessary; sometimes, we must do the unorthodox thing.

Typically, once I give the client the listings with their requested criteria, we only look at those properties. If they found anything outside of that (usually from one of the other real estate websites such as Zillow), I would suggest that they to do a drive-by first before scheduling a showing, and ninety-five percent of the time, there would be no need to schedule a showing. This can happen for several reasons—either it did not meet their criteria, it was not appealing, it was a for-sell-by-owner (FSBO), or it was not a legitimate listing. However, in this case, I met her at every property she wanted to view (we rode every animal on the merry-go-round, more than once). I did this so that she did not feel she was missing out on any possibilities; therefore, we left no stone unturned. Looking at houses was a pleasant distraction from all that she was going through, and it allowed me to check on her wellbeing. In the beginning, it was fun and exciting. One day someone dear to us both joined us at the park and rode the merry-go-round with us. We even stopped and got some refreshments.

Time was running out, still on the merry-go-round, making it to the Ferris wheel several times, only to have either the offer not accepted, or my client walked away because of the inspection report or other findings. This roundabout went on for a while. Then it happened! Our worst nightmare occurred! she became homeless! Her 30-day occupancy had expired on her existing home. At that point, she decided to move in with a family member as we continued to search for her Right Door. We were ready to get off the merry-go-round and leave the park; however, we knew that was not an option. We could not give up. Did I mention that this was during the winter season? The winter season is the slowest season for real estate sales. It also did not help that it was one of the worst winter seasons in Michigan, consisting of multiple snow-and-ice storms. We were hoping to find something soon because all day at the park in cold and snowy weather is not much fun. You just want to ride each ride at a minimum, then get out of there before you get frostbitten.

After many showings and submitting several offers that did not work out, a divorce, and becoming homeless, she finally found her Right Door, the house she would call her home. Of all the houses where she had submitted other offers, this one possessed her must-haves, those amenities that caused her to have the peace and security she wanted. The ride on the Ferris wheel was short and fun; we submitted an offer which was immediately accepted. Although the merry-go-round ride was (very) long, we made up for time on the roller coaster. After the inspection was completed, we negotiated a lower offer, and it was accepted without incidence (therefore, I did not have to go on the bumper car ride). Another time-saver was that we did not have to go through a lender's approval since this was a cash sale.

Although we were stuck on the merry-go-round longer than the norm, the visit to the amusement park was an adventure. There is always some enjoyment at an amusement park. We were able to view many houses, some from the listings and some that were not. Some of the houses were (very) interesting and different. The architect and updates of some were unexpected. For example, one house had a large circular fish tank that extended from the first floor to the basement. The basement entry was through spiral staircases on each side of the foyer; it also possessed one of my client's favorite amenities, an outdoor swimming pool. However, due to the maintenance, upkeep, and repairs needed, she decided to pass on that one (we discovered it was once owned and occupied by a local celebrity).

Then there were also several houses we viewed which just made me sad. The houses had been abused. Upon entering, you could smell the mold. There were flooded basements, leaking roofs, and even holes in the walls, where it looked like someone took a sledgehammer to it. I found this very disturbing, especially in those upscale neighborhoods.

Thinking about the closing day, I remember how cheerful everyone was—my client received the keys, the seller received the check, and although it was chilly that day, the sun was shining brightly as we exited the park. I remember being especially glad that we did not have to enter the house of mirrors (where distorted versions of Client IV could have shown up) because neither party confided in the reason for the divorce.

Although this was a long and daunting journey for Client IV, it all worked out in the end. She found her Right Door, where she continues to serve out her assignments. The bonus occurred less than four years later when her area's market value more than doubled—can't say the same for the other houses where her offers were not accepted.

CLIENT V - The Flood

I met Client V in a Bible class at the church where we both attended and became friends. One day Client V called me to say that she was selling her house and getting a divorce. Those are two of the top five stressors in life, and to go through them simultaneously is even more stressful. I knew if I would get any sleep during this process, I had to put on my whole armour, again! At our first meeting, she started the conversation by stating that she chose me as her agent because she needed someone she could trust, pray with, confide in, and lift her spirits during that difficult time. After signing all the documents and a lengthy conversation, we joined our faith together, in prayer, petitioning God for a victorious and expeditious outcome.

Once the property was listed, it was time to head to the amusement park. First ride, the merry-go-round, riding and hoping for an expeditious and fair offer. Two weeks after listing the property and multiple showings, one of the worst things that could go wrong happened—the basement flooded! Flooding water is one of the worst things that can happen to a house, and a seller's nightmare, especially when the cause is unknown. I had to suspend the showings by changing the listing to conditionally withdrawn. Conditionally withdrawn means that the property is still under contract with the listing agent but is temporarily not shown. Due to this unforeseen incident, we had to shut down the merry-go-round. We could either play the games or find a bench to sit on until the issue got resolved. Due to the other major issue that she was dealing with (the divorce), she chose to sit on the bench. After the inspection, the contractor reported that the flooding problem was more severe and more costly than expected. The repairs were completed after approximately three weeks, and the showings resumed (restarted the merry-go-round).

Before relisting the property, we also had to update the disclosure form to disclose the flooding issue (which could discourage buyers). However, we were fortunate that someone made an offer, at the asking price, within the first week of relisting the property. Onto the Ferris wheel! This ride was short and without incident. After accepting the offer and the contract signed, the inspection and appraisal reports were ordered. Time to board the roller coaster!

The inspection report came back with several items needing repair, including the plumbing work we thought was completed. In addition, the city inspector found violations that needed addressing; this caused more delay and more money. The ride on the roller coaster was getting intense and daunting; the buyers also had second thoughts about purchasing. Also, at this same time, Client V had filed for divorce and was nervously waiting for the court papers to be processed. To make matters more intense, Client V and her spouse were both residing in the house amid all the turmoil. Since she was the one that filed for the divorce, she felt that she was in a vulnerable position. Needless to say, this was a very intense and emotional time for her. As her agent and friend, I tried to support her in any way I could; we laughed, talked, and prayed a lot. I could only imagine the heaviness that she was going through. With all this adversity going on, the average person probably would have exploded by then. But, because of her faith and naturally kind and quiet spirit, she maintained her composure throughout it all.

Finally, after making all the necessary repairs, the initial buyer bought the house of their dreams, and the seller exited what was once her Right Door and entered her new Right Door. Many years later, she continues to enjoy the peace and comfort of her new life and continues to fulfill her assignments. Her trip to the park was rough initially, having to stop and start over, and the ride on the roller coaster was one of the most daunting and longest rides that one can experience. However, the bumper car ride was short and easy because the buyer's agent was honest and fair. There was no need for unnecessary negotiations. The buyer's agent was polite, confident, and knowledgeable, with over twenty-five years of experience. When we disagreed on certain items, her approach was to talk it out until we reached a mutual agreement that benefited both clients. Therefore, the bumper car was fun because we both played by the rules and negotiated professionally and ethically, resulting in a win-win situation. I am glad I met her early in my career because she set the road map for me to get a deal done with respect and integrity.

After the closing, we exited the park; we did not stop for cotton candy because she was still dealing with the divorce dilemma. However, we did celebrate later after all was said and done.

When times get tough, we must remind ourselves that whatever we are going through, it is only temporary, and this too shall pass; hold on to our faith (just like holding on to those handles on the roller coaster), because if we let go, we will fall. That is what my client did. She held on, and in the end, it all worked out—she walked out of what was once her Right Door and into her new Right Door, where she continues to serve out her purpose with peacefulness.

Client VI - Dual Expenses

Client VI is an acquaintance of mine that I met at church. One beautiful Autumn day, she contacted me to ask if I would sell her home. When I met with her, she told me that she had already moved out and rented an apartment. The dilemma was that she had an existing mortgage loan (on her home) and was now paying dual household expenses. My assignment was to sell her home ASAP to eliminate her having to pay two household expenses. Client VI stated that she wanted to sell her house "As Is." She did not want to list her home Federal Housing Administration (FHA) or Veteran Administration (VA) to avoid paying for or making any repairs to the property. I advised her, the problem with that was that the market in her area was, at least, seventy-five percent FHA buyers. Client VI is a prayer warrior and woman of great faith who insisted that we go forth, hoping that the twenty-five percent buyer was out there ready to purchase with cash or a conventional offer. As the agent, I was there to present the facts and give my suggestions, but optimally, it is the client's decision as to how they want to list their property, as long as it is within the real estate laws' guidelines and ethics. Therefore, we listed "As Is." Before entering the amusement park, she suggested we pray for an expeditious and victorious outcome.

Needless to say, we were stuck on the merry-go-round for months, receiving only FHA offers with contingencies requesting that the seller pay for all FHA-required repairs and also asking three-to-ten percent towards the closing cost. We received one cash offer from an investor that we did not accept because the offer was too low. Time was ticking; she continued to pay expenses for both residents. After several months, we entered the slow period (the winter season), where few to no offers were presented, and the few submitted were unacceptable. Still on the merry-go-round and believing, by faith, that eventually the right offer would be submitted so that we could exit this ride.

Because of her faith, Client VI did not panic during the silent time. Instead, we continued to encourage one another with prayer and positivity. Finally, I suggested that if she had the money to make the FHA, required repairs, we could add the FHA/VA financial criteria to the listing, which would increase her chances of getting an acceptable offer. She agreed, but after that I did not hear from her for several weeks. After not hearing from her, I called to ask her what was going on. She mentioned that she was applying for a loan to make the repairs. Nooo!!! I told her that's the last thing she should do; if she didn't have the cash to make the repairs, we would keep the listing "As Is." She thanked me for the suggestion and stated that something did not feel right when she attempted to take out the loan. I explained that she probably felt that way because she was about to board the roller coaster unnecessarily by adding more debt and stress to the situation.

I'm glad I contacted her before that train left the station (before she committed to the loan) because, within twenty-four hours, something happened—the ram in the bush! The investor who made the cash offer earlier called back and made an offer that was acceptable to the seller. Although the offer was below the asking price, the seller stated that she was ready to close that chapter of her life and move on with peace of mind. Off the merry-go-round! Onto the Ferris wheel! This ride was very short, making up for the lengthy merry-go-round ride.

Boarding the roller coaster! Since this was a cash offer, the ride should have been one time around and off; however, we had to ride several more rounds in this case. The reason for this is that the investor almost backed out of the agreement. He wanted to reduce the offer price midway to closing. This is where I had to leave Client VI on the roller coaster and head over to the bumper car ride. With my client's permission, I told him no deal to the lesser offer. If he could not honor the agreed-upon offer, I would prepare a mutual release of the contract. My client and I were ready to relist the property and re-start the merry-go-round. Within an hour of this suggestion, he phoned back to say he was ready to go forward with the initial agreement. I met with my client as she got off the roller coaster, and we headed to the closing. Before leaving the park, we stopped for cotton candy and ice cream.

Initially, I did not feel great that Client VI had to sell below market price. I even asked her several times if she was sure about the offer before we fully committed. I did this because I wanted to be sure that she did not feel pressured and regret her decision later. She told me that she had prayed about it and that her peace of mind was more important than the money. That statement was my confirmation to proceed without feeling that I had not done all I could do as her Realtor.

In the end, it all worked out. Client VI walked away with a generous check and peace of mind. My lesson from this was that my wellbeing and peace of mind are as good as my client's wellbeing and peace of mind.

Realtors, I know that we are taught that we should always try to get the maximum from an offer to be successful. While this is true, I like to add, to be successful is always to know that you did your best for your client, and the greatest reward is knowing that in the end, your client was satisfied and had peace with their outcome. Therefore, I continue to communicate with Client VI. Each time we talk, she loves talking about the experience we shared when selling her house, how happy she was with the results, how she is enjoying her new life, and how she will refer me to everyone she knows, which she has.

Client VII - The Foreclosure

I began this case in the initial stage of the onerous COVID-19 Virus, which eventually swept the nation. In March 2020, I watched the local news report of the first COVID-19 case in Oakland County, Michigan. I immediately grew concerned because I live in Oakland County, and the gym I attended was also located in Oakland County. Therefore, the following day, I reluctantly went to the gym to attend my yoga class (in a closed-off room inside the gym). After arriving at my class, I felt paranoid and annoyed whenever someone would cough, plus the instructor was MIA (missing-in-action). Finally, about fifteen minutes later, someone came in and announced that the instructor would not be in due to an illness; they went on to describe how terrible she sounded when she called in. Well, that was the final warning for me. I knew I would not be back anytime soon. I also decided not to accept any real estate assignments until this virus crisis has passed.

However, several days later, I received a phone call from Client VII who stated that she was referred to me by her sister-in-law. She stated that her house was going into foreclosure in about a month. Her sister-in-law told her if anyone could assist her in selling it before then, it would be Angela (clearly, her sister-in-law had more confidence in me than I did in myself). I told her I would have to think and pray about it and give her a call the next day. Before ending the call, she explained more about her situation. I could hear the desperation in her voice. The next day, I called Client VII and told her that I would take her case.

I met with Client VII later that day to sign the listing documents. Upon meeting, she informed me that her husband had passed away a year ago, and before his passing, he took out a Reverse Mortgage on the house. "A Reverse Mortgage is a mortgage loan, usually secured by a residential property, that enables the borrower to access the unencumbered value of the property. The loans are typically promoted to older homeowners and typically do not require monthly mortgage payments. Borrowers are still responsible for **property taxes** and **homeowner's insurance**. Reverse mortgages allow elders to access the **home equity** they have built up in their homes now and defer payment of the loan until they die, sell, or move out of the house. Because there are no required mortgage payments on a reverse mortgage, the **interest** is added to the loan balance each month. The rising loan balance can eventually grow to exceed the home's value, particularly in times of declining home values or if the borrower continues to live in the home for many years. However, the borrower (or the borrower's estate) is generally not required to repay any additional loan balance in excess of the value of the home." - **Wikipedia**

Since Client VII had not paid on the mortgage within the year of her husband's death, the house was scheduled to go into foreclosure in April 2020; therefore, we had approximately five weeks to find a buyer and close on the property before the foreclosure. Because the property was located in an affluent suburban neighborhood with low inventory and high demand, this should not be a problem, or should it?

The amusement park trip would have to be rushed, on and off, the rides before the park closed (before the government order a shut down). I could tell how my confidence had grown over the years as a Realtor. I experienced no anxiety over the situation and slept each night soundly. I attribute this to experience. Knowing that once I have done all that I can do (in the natural) for my client (including prayer), in the end, it will all work out. However, I was extra cautious due to the COVID virus, which had begun to spread. Every day the news reported updates and alerts regarding the virus. They also reported that we should wash our hands and use sanitizer frequently, and wear masks.

Along with the foreclosure dilemma, the house needed some repairs, including a roof; also, approximately seventy percent of the market were FHA Buyers. This was going to be a challenge because there was no time to make the repairs, nor did Client VII have the funds to make them; therefore, we had to list the property "As Is" with cash or conventional terms. We were flooded with offers within two weeks; however, as expected, they were all FHAs—stuck on the merry-go-round!

After approximately two weeks from listing the property, we received an offer from an investor. Yea! Off the merry-go-round, onto the Ferris wheel! Time was ticking; the park was about to close. We had three weeks to close on the property before it went into foreclosure. This was possible with the cash offer (only if everything went as expected and in a timely manner). By mid-March, the COVID-19 virus had swamped the State of Michigan—thousands of people had been afflicted, and hundreds had lost their lives. We could not close until the inspection and appraisal were completed. Therefore, we boarded the roller coaster, the inspection and appraisal were ordered and completed within a week. After the inspection results came back, the buyer wanted to amend the contract to lower the offer price because the roof needed replacing. Usually, I would have had time to negotiate or even have my client walk away from the deal and relist the property, but we had no time for this under the circumstances. I had no time to go on the bumper car ride with the buyer's agent. We accepted the reduced offer (which wasn't much).

The following Monday, the governor ordered a shutdown on non-essential business. Because of this ordinance, the Board of Realtors for the State of Michigan mandated that no real estate activities take place until the ordinance had been lifted. The mandate stated that Realtors could not enter any occupied residence; we were, however, allowed to close out any active cases that we were working on at the time. During this time, there were daily news reports on the rapid changes in the real estate market. Buyers were permitted to opt-out of their contract agreements and walk away without losing their earnest money deposits. Many buyers were taking advantage of this since they were not allowed on the occupied properties' premises. During this time, a week had passed, and I had not heard from the buyer's agent; therefore, I thought they were going to back out of the contract. Still stuck on the roller coaster, the ride began to get a bit rocky and bumpy. Client VII became concerned and asked what was going on, why we hadn't heard from the buyer's agent. I explained that she was on the roller coaster ride and what that meant. Sometimes, right before the closing, it can get a bit quiet. Typically, this occurs because the title company is preparing their documents, and the buyer is working things out on their end with the lender and securing their funds, so buckle up, hold on tight, pray and enjoy the ride; it'll soon be over. She asked, "Are you on this ride with me"? I answered, "I sure am, sitting right beside you."

It was now a little more than a week before the foreclosure date. The next day I received a call from the title company, stating that they needed a particular document from the seller, and without it, we could not get a clear-to-close. When I asked Client VII about the document, she stated that the president of her Homeowners Association (HOA) had the document, and she would get it to me the next day. However, the next day she still could not get the document because the president was afraid of coming in contact with anyone because of the COVID virus. Because the virus was new and in the initial stage, people were confused and afraid. I suggested that she request the president to leave the document on her porch and let her know that we cannot get a clear-to-close without it. The next day, the president left the document on the porch, Client VII submitted it to me, and I forwarded it to the title company. The following day, we received a clear-to-close and were able to secure a closing date.

The closing date was March 31st, whoosh!!! We made it! Off the roller coaster! Just days before the foreclosure was to have taken place. Usually, I would meet my client at the closing, and, typically, the other agent and their client are present too (the agents are there to support the client and pick up a copy of the closing documents and the commission check). However, because of the devastation of the pandemic, this closing was different. Agents were not allowed to accompany their clients to the closing, and each client had to meet separately. Also, to enter the building of the title company, each person had to sign an electronic form the day before and submit it to the title company before entering the building. There were three questions on the form: 1) Have you returned from out of the country within the last three months? 2) Have you had the COVID-19 virus? 3) have you been around anyone with the virus? If the answer to all three questions were no, you were allowed to enter the building. The buyer and seller met one-on-one with the Closer at separate title companies. I came later, after the closing, to pick up my package.

Leaving the park was different that day; usually, when leaving the park after the closing, there's a shaking of hands and congratulatory conversations going on as we exit the gate. However, this day everyone left separately. It was the first time I did not walk out with my client. There was no stopping for cotton candy, and after the park closed, a sign went up that read, "Closed Until Further Notice."

CONCLUSION

In conclusion, do not be like the children of Israel, who wandered in the wilderness for forty years because they didn't obey God when He told them to take their land. Your land is your home; it is the place where God wants you to be at a specific time in your life. He wants you to enter the Right Door so that you will have peace in your life and, thereby, be in position to carry out the purpose He has planned for you through your assignments. This book talks about the Right Door as it pertains to your home; however, the Right Door is also anywhere, anything, or anyone you are entering or exiting throughout your life.

Also, have faith that things will turn out the way they are supposed to in the end. Your experiences and journeys in life are only temporary, so try to find joy in them. Someone once said that "Life is ten percent of what happens to you and ninety percent of how you respond to it." Someone else once said, "When you get to the point that you are not experiencing any of life's issues, it might be that you are no longer here." That day is inevitable to us all, but until then, get God in your life, and in all thy getting, get joy and peace. And when it's all said and done, if you are blessed with the opportunity to meet your Heavenly Father, He's not going to ask how much money you made throughout your life's journey, but, rather, how did you treat the people you encountered along the way?

ACKNOWLEDGEMENTS

Angela Bean has been an Associate Broker with North American Real Estate for several years. Our company's true values rely on our ethics, integrity, morals, and client relationships. Angela epitomizes our true core values, unlike anyone that has ever walked through our doors! The honesty and compassion she shares enable her to be successful in all aspects of life! - **Anthony Cartwright, Owner, North American Real Estate**

Heaven sent, and spirit led! Angela listens to your desires and uses her vast knowledge to assist with finding the best place for you. She is thoughtful, kind, prompt, and courteous in her approach always. No drama, pressure, or hassles! A place to call your own, your happiness, and your security matter to Angela Bean!! - **Belinda and Keith Tucker**

Angie, I would like to thank you for this opportunity to write a few lines to thank you for riding the "roller coaster" of faith with me during the challenges we faced during the selling of my home. Your faithfulness, integrity, and knowledge are surpassed only by our Lord and Savior, Jesus Christ, which I know sent you as my angel to help get me across the finish line. May God continue to use you as his vessel to enlighten his children of the pitfalls awaiting us as we continue to deal with this Babylonian system. - **Penny F.**

As iron sharpens iron, so one person sharpens another,

so it is with Angela. She is compassionate, knowledgeable, and a wonderful friend. I have been able to grow in many areas of my life because of Angela, and she was there for me when I suddenly had to sell my house. - **Anonymous**

Sales are Music to the Ears! We know successful sales don't just happen- they are orchestrated. Good job, maestro! - unknown author

CODE OF ETHICS & STANDARDS OF PRACTICE

Preamble

Under all is the land. Upon its wise utilization and widely allocated ownership depend the survival and growth of free institutions and of our civilization. REALTORS® should recognize that the interests of the nation and its citizens require the highest and best use of the land and the widest distribution of land ownership. They require the creation of adequate housing, the building of functioning cities, the development of productive industries and farms, and the preservation of a healthful environment.

Such interests impose obligations beyond those of ordinary commerce. They impose grave social responsibility and a patriotic duty to which REALTORS® should dedicate themselves, and for which they should be diligent in preparing themselves. REALTORS®, therefore, are zealous to maintain and improve the standards of their calling and share with their fellow REALTORS® a common responsibility for its integrity and honor.

In recognition and appreciation of their obligations to clients, customers, the public, and each other, REALTORS® continuously strive to become and remain informed on issues affecting real estate and, as knowledgeable professionals, they willingly share the fruit of their experience and study with others. They identify and take steps, through enforcement of this Code of Ethics and by assisting appropriate regulatory bodies, to eliminate practices which may damage the public or which might discredit or bring dishonor to the real estate profession. REALTORS® having direct personal knowledge of conduct that may violate the Code of Ethics involving misappropriation of client or customer funds or property, willful discrimination, or fraud resulting in substantial economic harm, bring such matters to the attention of the appropriate Board or Association of REALTORS®. *(Amended 1/00)*

Realizing that cooperation with other real estate professionals promotes the best interests of those who utilize their services, REALTORS® urge exclusive representation of clients; do not attempt to gain any unfair advantage over their competitors; and they refrain from making unsolicited comments about other practitioners. In instances where their opinion is sought, or where REALTORS® believe that comment is necessary, their opinion is offered in an objective, professional manner, uninfluenced by any personal motivation or potential advantage or gain.

The term REALTOR® has come to connote competency, fairness, and high integrity resulting from adherence to a lofty ideal of moral conduct in business relations. No inducement of profit and no instruction from clients ever can justify departure from this ideal.

In the interpretation of this obligation, REALTORS® can take no safer guide than that which has been handed down through the centuries, embodied in the Golden Rule, "Whatsoever ye would that others should do to you, do ye even so to them."

Accepting this standard as their own, REALTORS® pledge to observe its spirit in all of their activities whether conducted personally, through associates or others, or via technological means, and to conduct their business in accordance with the tenets set forth below. *(Amended 1/07)*

Duties to Clients and Customers

Article 1 (Case Interpretations for Article 1)

When representing a buyer, seller, landlord, tenant, or other client as an agent, REALTORS® pledge themselves to protect and promote the interests of their client. This obligation to the client is primary, but it does not relieve REALTORS® of their obligation to treat all parties honestly. When serving a buyer, seller, landlord, tenant or other party in a non-agency capacity, REALTORS® remain obligated to treat all parties honestly. *(Amended 1/01)*

- Standard of Practice 1-1

REALTORS®, when acting as principals in a real estate transaction, remain obligated by the duties imposed by the Code of Ethics. *(Amended 1/93)*

- Standard of Practice 1-2

The duties imposed by the Code of Ethics encompass all real estate-related activities and transactions whether conducted in person, electronically, or through any other means.

The duties the Code of Ethics imposes are applicable whether REALTORS® are acting as agents or in legally recognized non-agency capacities except that any duty imposed exclusively on agents by law or regulation shall not be imposed by this Code of Ethics on REALTORS® acting in non-agency capacities.

As used in this Code of Ethics, "client" means the person(s) or entity(ies) with whom a REALTOR® or a REALTOR®'s firm has an agency or legally recognized non-agency relationship; "customer" means a party to a real estate transaction who receives information, services, or benefits but has no contractual relationship with the REALTOR® or the REALTOR®'s firm; "prospect" means a purchaser, seller, tenant, or landlord who is not subject to a representation relationship with the REALTOR® or REALTOR®'s firm; "agent" means a real estate licensee (including brokers and sales associates) acting in an agency relationship as defined by state law or regulation; and "broker" means a real estate licensee (including brokers and sales associates) acting as an agent or in a legally recognized non-agency capacity. *(Adopted 1/95, Amended 1/07)*

- Standard of Practice 1-3

REALTORS®, in attempting to secure a listing, shall not deliberately mislead the owner as to market value.

- Standard of Practice 1-4

REALTORS®, when seeking to become a buyer/tenant representative, shall not mislead buyers or tenants as to savings or other benefits that might be realized through use of the REALTOR®'s services. *(Amended 1/93)*

- Standard of Practice 1-5

REALTORS® may represent the seller/landlord and buyer/tenant in the same transaction only after full disclosure to and with informed consent of both parties. *(Adopted 1/93)*

- Standard of Practice 1-6

REALTORS® shall submit offers and counter-offers objectively and as quickly as possible. *(Adopted 1/93, Amended 1/95)*

- Standard of Practice 1-7

When acting as listing brokers, REALTORS® shall continue to submit to the seller/landlord all offers and counter-offers until closing or execution of a lease unless the seller/landlord has waived this obligation in writing. Upon the written request of a cooperating broker who submits an offer to the listing broker, the listing broker shall provide, as soon as practical, a written affirmation to the cooperating broker stating that the offer has been submitted to the seller/landlord, or a written notification that the seller/ landlord has waived the obligation to have the offer presented. REALTORS® shall not be obligated to continue to market the property after an offer has been accepted by the seller/landlord. REALTORS® shall recommend that sellers/landlords obtain the advice of legal counsel prior to acceptance of a subsequent offer except where the acceptance is contingent on the termination of the pre-existing purchase contract or lease. *(Amended 1/20)*

- Standard of Practice 1-8

REALTORS® , acting as agents or brokers of buyers/tenants, shall submit to buyers/tenants all offers and counter-offers until acceptance but have no obligation to continue to show properties to their clients after an offer has been accepted unless otherwise agreed in writing. REALTORS®, acting as agents or brokers of buyers/tenants, shall recommend that buyers/tenants obtain the advice of legal counsel if there is a question as to whether a pre-existing contract has been terminated. *(Adopted 1/93, Amended 1/99)*

- Standard of Practice 1-9

The obligation of REALTORS® to preserve confidential information (as defined by state law) provided by their clients in the course of any agency relationship or non-agency relationship recognized by law continues after termination of agency relationships or any non-agency relationships recognized by law. REALTORS® shall not knowingly, during or following the termination of professional relationships with their clients:

- reveal confidential information of clients; or
- use confidential information of clients to the disadvantage of clients; or
- use confidential information of clients for the REALTOR®'s advantage or the advantage of third parties unless:
- clients consent after full disclosure; or

- REALTORS® are required by court order; or
- it is the intention of a client to commit a crime and the information is necessary to prevent the crime; or
- it is necessary to defend a REALTOR® or the REALTOR®'s employees or associates against an accusation of wrongful conduct.

Information concerning latent material defects is not considered confidential information under this Code of Ethics. *(Adopted 1/93, Amended 1/01)*

- Standard of Practice 1-10

REALTORS® shall, consistent with the terms and conditions of their real estate licensure and their property management agreement, competently manage the property of clients with due regard for the rights, safety and health of tenants and others lawfully on the premises. *(Adopted 1/95, Amended 1/00)*

- Standard of Practice 1-11

REALTORS® who are employed to maintain or manage a client's property shall exercise due diligence and make reasonable efforts to protect it against reasonably foreseeable contingencies and losses. *(Adopted 1/95)*

- Standard of Practice 1-12

When entering into listing contracts, REALTORS® must advise sellers/landlords of:

- the REALTOR®'s company policies regarding cooperation and the amount(s) of any compensation that will be offered to subagents, buyer/tenant agents, and/or brokers acting in legally recognized non-agency capacities;
- the fact that buyer/tenant agents or brokers, even if compensated by listing brokers, or by sellers/landlords may represent the interests of buyers/tenants; and
- any potential for listing brokers to act as disclosed dual agents, e.g. buyer/tenant agents. *(Adopted 1/93, Renumbered 1/98, Amended 1/03)*
- Standard of Practice 1-13

When entering into buyer/tenant agreements, REALTORS® must advise potential clients of:

- the REALTOR®'s company policies regarding cooperation;
- the amount of compensation to be paid by the client;
- the potential for additional or offsetting compensation from other brokers, from the seller or landlord, or from other parties;
- any potential for the buyer/tenant representative to act as a disclosed dual agent, e.g. listing broker, subagent, landlord's agent, etc., and
- the possibility that sellers or sellers' representatives may not treat the existence, terms, or conditions of offers as

confidential unless confidentiality is required by law, regulation, or by any confidentiality agreement between the parties. *(Adopted 1/93, Renumbered 1/98, Amended 1/06)*

- Standard of Practice 1-14

Fees for preparing appraisals or other valuations shall not be contingent upon the amount of the appraisal or valuation. *(Adopted 1/02)*

- Standard of Practice 1-15

REALTORS®, in response to inquiries from buyers or cooperating brokers shall, with the sellers' approval, disclose the existence of offers on the property. Where disclosure is authorized, REALTORS® shall also disclose, if asked, whether offers were obtained by the listing licensee, another licensee in the listing firm, or by a cooperating broker. *(Adopted 1/03, Amended 1/09)*

- Standard of Practice 1-16

REALTORS® shall not access or use, or permit or enable others to access or use, listed or managed property on terms or conditions other than those authorized by the owner or seller. *(Adopted 1/12)*

Article 2 (Case Interpretations for Article 2)

REALTORS® shall avoid exaggeration, misrepresentation, or concealment of pertinent facts relating to the property or the transaction. REALTORS® shall not, however, be obligated to discover latent defects in the property, to advise on matters outside the scope of their real estate license, or to disclose facts which are confidential under the scope of agency or non-agency relationships as defined by state law. *(Amended 1/00)*

- Standard of Practice 2-1

REALTORS® shall only be obligated to discover and disclose adverse factors reasonably apparent to someone with expertise in those areas required by their real estate licensing authority. Article 2 does not impose upon the REALTOR® the obligation of expertise in other professional or technical disciplines. *(Amended 1/96)*

- Standard of Practice 2-2

(Renumbered as Standard of Practice 1-12 1/98)

- Standard of Practice 2-3

(Renumbered as Standard of Practice 1-13 1/98)

- Standard of Practice 2-4

REALTORS® shall not be parties to the naming of a false consideration in any document, unless it be the naming of an obviously nominal consideration.

- Standard of Practice 2-5

Factors defined as "non-material" by law or regulation or which are expressly referenced in law or regulation as not being subject to disclosure are considered not "pertinent" for purposes of Article 2. *(Adopted 1/93)*

Article 3 (Case Interpretations for Article 3)

REALTORS® shall cooperate with other brokers except when cooperation is not in the client's best interest. The obligation to cooperate does not include the obligation to share commissions, fees, or to otherwise compensate another broker. *(Amended 1/95)*

- Standard of Practice 3-1

REALTORS®, acting as exclusive agents or brokers of sellers/ landlords, establish the terms and conditions of offers to cooperate. Unless expressly indicated in offers to cooperate, cooperating brokers may not assume that the offer of cooperation includes an offer of compensation. Terms of compensation, if any, shall be ascertained by cooperating brokers before beginning efforts to accept the offer of cooperation. *(Amended 1/99)*

- Standard of Practice 3-2

Any change in compensation offered for cooperative services must be communicated to the other REALTOR® prior to the time that REALTOR® submits an offer to purchase/lease the property. After a REALTOR® has submitted an offer to purchase or lease property, the listing broker may not attempt to unilaterally modify the offered compensation with respect to that cooperative transaction. *(Amended 1/14)*

- Standard of Practice 3-3

Standard of Practice 3-2 does not preclude the listing broker and cooperating broker from entering into an agreement to change cooperative compensation. *(Adopted 1/94)*

- Standard of Practice 3-4

REALTORS®, acting as listing brokers, have an affirmative obligation to disclose the existence of dual or variable rate commission arrangements (i.e., listings where one amount of commission is payable if the listing broker's firm is the procuring cause of sale/lease and a different amount of commission is payable if the sale/lease results through the efforts of the seller/ landlord or a cooperating broker). The listing broker shall, as soon as practical, disclose the existence of such arrangements to potential cooperating brokers and shall, in response to inquiries from cooperating brokers, disclose the differential that would result in a cooperative transaction or in a sale/lease that results through the efforts of the seller/landlord. If the cooperating broker is a buyer/tenant representative, the buyer/tenant representative must disclose such information to their client before the client makes an offer to purchase or lease. *(Amended 1/02)*

- Standard of Practice 3-5

It is the obligation of subagents to promptly disclose all pertinent facts to the principal's agent prior to as well as after a purchase or lease agreement is executed. *(Amended 1/93)*

- Standard of Practice 3-6

REALTORS® shall disclose the existence of accepted offers, including offers with unresolved contingencies, to any broker seeking cooperation. *(Adopted 5/86, Amended 1/04)*

- Standard of Practice 3-7

When seeking information from another REALTOR® concerning property under a management or listing agreement, REALTORS® shall disclose their REALTOR® status and whether their interest is personal or on behalf of a client and, if on behalf of a client, their relationship with the client. *(Amended 1/11)*

- Standard of Practice 3-8

REALTORS® shall not misrepresent the availability of access to show or inspect a listed property. *(Amended 11/87)*

- Standard of Practice 3-9

REALTORS® shall not provide access to listed property on terms other than those established by the owner or the listing broker. *(Adopted 1/10)*

- Standard of Practice 3-10

The duty to cooperate established in Article 3 relates to the obligation to share information on listed property, and to make property available to other brokers for showing to prospective purchasers/tenants when it is in the best interests of sellers/landlords. *(Adopted 1/11)*

- Standard of Practice 3-11

REALTORS® may not refuse to cooperate on the basis of a broker's race, color, religion, sex, handicap, familial status, national origin, sexual orientation, or gender identity. *(Adopted 1/20)*

Article 4 (Case Interpretations for Article 4)

REALTORS® shall not acquire an interest in or buy or present offers from themselves, any member of their immediate families, their firms or any member thereof, or any entities in which they have any ownership interest, any real property without making their true position known to the owner or the owner's agent or broker. In selling property they own, or in which they have any interest, REALTORS® shall reveal their ownership or interest in writing to the purchaser or the purchaser's representative. *(Amended 1/00)*

- Standard of Practice 4-1

For the protection of all parties, the disclosures required by Article 4 shall be in writing and provided by REALTORS® prior to the signing of any contract. *(Adopted 2/86)*

Article 5 (Case Interpretations for Article 5)

REALTORS® shall not undertake to provide professional services concerning a property or its value where they have a present or contemplated interest unless such interest is specifically disclosed to all affected parties.

Article 6 (Case Interpretations for Article 6)

REALTORS® shall not accept any commission, rebate, or profit on expenditures made for their client, without the client's knowledge and consent.

When recommending real estate products or services (e.g., homeowner's insurance, warranty programs, mortgage financing, title insurance, etc.), REALTORS® shall disclose to the client or customer to whom the recommendation is made any financial benefits or fees, other than real estate referral fees, the REALTOR® or REALTOR®'s firm may receive as a direct result of such recommendation. *(Amended 1/99)*

- Standard of Practice 6-1

REALTORS® shall not recommend or suggest to a client or a customer the use of services of another organization or business entity in which they have a direct interest without disclosing such interest at the time of the recommendation or suggestion. *(Amended 5/88)*

Article 7 (Case Interpretations for Article 7)

In a transaction, REALTORS® shall not accept compensation from more than one party, even if permitted by law, without disclosure to all parties and the informed consent of the REALTOR®'s client or clients. *(Amended 1/93)*

Article 8 (Case Interpretations for Article 8)

REALTORS® shall keep in a special account in an appropriate financial institution, separated from their own funds, monies coming into their possession in trust for other persons, such as escrows, trust funds, clients' monies, and other like items.

Article 9 (Case Interpretations for Article 9)

REALTORS®, for the protection of all parties, shall assure whenever possible that all agreements related to real estate transactions including, but not limited to, listing and representation agreements, purchase contracts, and leases are in writing in clear and understandable language expressing the specific terms, conditions, obligations and commitments of the parties. A copy of each agreement shall be furnished to each party to such agreements upon their signing or initialing. *(Amended 1/04)*

- Standard of Practice 9-1

For the protection of all parties, REALTORS® shall use reasonable care to ensure that documents pertaining to the purchase, sale, or lease of real estate are kept current through the use of written extensions or amendments. *(Amended 1/93)*

- Standard of Practice 9-2

When assisting or enabling a client or customer in establishing a contractual relationship (e.g., listing and representation agreements, purchase agreements, leases, etc.) electronically, REALTORS® shall make reasonable efforts to explain the nature and disclose the specific terms of the contractual relationship being established prior to it being agreed to by a contracting party. *(Adopted 1/07)*

Duties to the Public

Article 10 (Case Interpretations for Article 10)

REALTORS® shall not deny equal professional services to any person for reasons of race, color, religion, sex, handicap, familial status, national origin, sexual orientation, or gender identity. REALTORS® shall not be parties to any plan or agreement to discriminate against a person or persons on the basis of race, color, religion, sex, handicap, familial status, national origin, sexual orientation, or gender identity. *(Amended 1/14)*

REALTORS®, in their real estate employment practices, shall not discriminate against any person or persons on the basis of race, color, religion, sex, handicap, familial status, national origin, sexual orientation, or gender identity. *(Amended 1/14)*

- Standard of Practice 10-1

When involved in the sale or lease of a residence, REALTORS® shall not volunteer information regarding the racial, religious or ethnic composition of any neighborhood nor shall they engage in any activity which may result in panic selling, however, REALTORS® may provide other demographic information. *(Adopted 1/94, Amended 1/06)*

- Standard of Practice 10-2

When not involved in the sale or lease of a residence, REALTORS® may provide demographic information related to a property, transaction or professional assignment to a party if such demographic information is (a) deemed by the REALTOR® to be needed to assist with or complete, in a manner consistent with Article 10, a real estate transaction or professional assignment and (b) is obtained or derived from a recognized, reliable, independent, and impartial source. The source of such information and any additions, deletions, modifications, interpretations, or other changes shall be disclosed in reasonable detail. *(Adopted 1/05, Renumbered 1/06)*

- Standard of Practice 10-3

REALTORS® shall not print, display or circulate any statement or advertisement with respect to selling or renting of a property that indicates any preference, limitations or discrimination based on race, color, religion, sex, handicap, familial status, national origin, sexual orientation, or gender identity. *(Adopted 1/94, Renumbered 1/05 and 1/06, Amended 1/14)*

- Standard of Practice 10-4

As used in Article 10 "real estate employment practices" relates to employees and independent contractors providing real estate-related services and the administrative and clerical staff directly supporting those individuals. *(Adopted 1/00, Renumbered 1/05 and 1/06)*

- Standard of Practice 10-5

REALTORS® must not use harassing speech, hate speech, epithets, or slurs based on race, color, religion, sex, handicap, familial status, national origin, sexual orientation, or gender identity. *(Adopted and Effective 11/2020)*

Article 11 (Case Interpretations for Article 11)

The services which REALTORS® provide to their clients and customers shall conform to the standards of practice and competence which are reasonably expected in the specific real estate disciplines in which they engage; specifically, residential real estate brokerage, real property management, commercial and industrial real estate brokerage, land brokerage, real estate appraisal, real estate counseling, real estate syndication, real estate auction, and international real estate.

REALTORS® shall not undertake to provide specialized professional services concerning a type of property or service that is outside their field of competence unless they engage the assistance of one who is competent on such types of property or service, or unless the facts are fully disclosed to the client. Any persons engaged to provide such assistance shall be so identified to the client and their contribution to the assignment should be set forth. *(Amended 1/10)*

- Standard of Practice 11-1

When REALTORS® prepare opinions of real property value or price they must:

- be knowledgeable about the type of property being valued,
- have access to the information and resources necessary to formulate an accurate opinion, and

- be familiar with the area where the subject property is located

unless lack of any of these is disclosed to the party requesting the opinion in advance.

When an opinion of value or price is prepared other than in pursuit of a listing or to assist a potential purchaser in formulating a purchase offer, the opinion shall include the following unless the party requesting the opinion requires a specific type of report or different data set:

- identification of the subject property
- date prepared
- defined value or price
- limiting conditions, including statements of purpose(s) and intended user(s)
- any present or contemplated interest, including the possibility of representing the seller/landlord or buyers/tenants
- basis for the opinion, including applicable market data
- if the opinion is not an appraisal, a statement to that effect
- disclosure of whether and when a physical inspection of the property's exterior was conducted
- disclosure of whether and when a physical inspection of the property's interior was conducted

- disclosure of whether the REALTOR® has any conflicts of interest *(Amended 1/14)*

- Standard of Practice 11-2

The obligations of the Code of Ethics in respect of real estate disciplines other than appraisal shall be interpreted and applied in accordance with the standards of competence and practice which clients and the public reasonably require to protect their rights and interests considering the complexity of the transaction, the availability of expert assistance, and, where the REALTOR® is an agent or subagent, the obligations of a fiduciary. *(Adopted 1/95)*

- Standard of Practice 11-3

When REALTORS® provide consultive services to clients which involve advice or counsel for a fee (not a commission), such advice shall be rendered in an objective manner and the fee shall not be contingent on the substance of the advice or counsel given. If brokerage or transaction services are to be provided in addition to consultive services, a separate compensation may be paid with prior agreement between the client and REALTOR®. *(Adopted 1/96)*

- Standard of Practice 11-4

The competency required by Article 11 relates to services contracted for between REALTORS® and their clients or customers; the duties expressly imposed by the Code of Ethics; and the duties imposed by law or regulation. *(Adopted 1/02)*

Article 12 (Case Interpretations for Article 12)

REALTORS® shall be honest and truthful in their real estate communications and shall present a true picture in their advertising, marketing, and other representations. REALTORS® shall ensure that their status as real estate professionals is readily apparent in their advertising, marketing, and other representations, and that the recipients of all real estate communications are, or have been, notified that those communications are from a real estate professional. *(Amended 1/08)*

- Standard of Practice 12-1

Unless they are receiving no compensation from any source for their time and services, REALTORS® may use the term "free" and similar terms in their advertising and in other representations only if they clearly and conspicuously disclose:

1) by whom they are being, or expect to be, paid;
2) the amount of the payment or anticipated payment;
3) any conditions associated with the payment, offered product or service, and;
4) any other terms relating to their compensation. *(Amended 1/20)*

- Standard of Practice 12-2

Deleted (1/20)

- Standard of Practice 12-3

The offering of premiums, prizes, merchandise discounts or other inducements to list, sell, purchase, or lease is not, in itself, unethical even if receipt of the benefit is contingent on listing, selling, purchasing, or leasing through the REALTOR® making the offer. However, REALTORS® must exercise care and candor in any such advertising or other public or private representations so that any party interested in receiving or otherwise benefiting from the REALTOR®'s offer will have clear, thorough, advance understanding of all the terms and conditions of the offer. The offering of any inducements to do business is subject to the limitations and restrictions of state law and the ethical obligations established by any applicable Standard of Practice. *(Amended 1/95)*

- Standard of Practice 12-4

REALTORS® shall not offer for sale/lease or advertise property without authority. When acting as listing brokers or as subagents, REALTORS® shall not quote a price different from that agreed upon with the seller/landlord. *(Amended 1/93)*

- Standard of Practice 12-5

Realtors® shall not advertise nor permit any person employed by or affiliated with them to advertise real estate services or listed property in any medium (e.g., electronically, print, radio, television, etc.) without disclosing the name of that Realtor®'s firm in a reasonable and readily apparent manner either in the advertisement or in electronic advertising via a link to a display with all required disclosures. *(Adopted 11/86, Amended 1/16)*

- Standard of Practice 12-6

REALTORS®, when advertising unlisted real property for sale/lease in which they have an ownership interest, shall disclose their status as both owners/landlords and as REALTORS® or real estate licensees. *(Amended 1/93)*

- Standard of Practice 12-7

Only REALTORS® who participated in the transaction as the listing broker or cooperating broker (selling broker) may claim to have "sold" the property. Prior to closing, a cooperating broker may post a "sold" sign only with the consent of the listing broker. *(Amended 1/96)*

- Standard of Practice 12-8

The obligation to present a true picture in representations to the public includes information presented, provided, or displayed on REALTORS®' websites. REALTORS® shall use reasonable efforts to ensure that information on their websites is current. When it becomes apparent that information on a REALTOR®'s website is no longer current or accurate, REALTORS® shall promptly take corrective action. *(Adopted 1/07)*

- Standard of Practice 12-9

REALTOR® firm websites shall disclose the firm's name and state(s) of licensure in a reasonable and readily apparent manner.

Websites of REALTORS® and non-member licensees affiliated with a REALTOR® firm shall disclose the firm's name and that REALTOR®'s or non-member licensee's state(s) of licensure in a reasonable and readily apparent manner. *(Adopted 1/07)*

- Standard of Practice 12-10

REALTORS®' obligation to present a true picture in their advertising and representations to the public includes Internet content, images, and the URLs and domain names they use, and prohibits REALTORS® from:

- engaging in deceptive or unauthorized framing of real estate brokerage websites;
- manipulating (e.g., presenting content developed by others) listing and other content in any way that produces a deceptive or misleading result;
- deceptively using metatags, keywords or other devices/methods to direct, drive, or divert Internet traffic; or
- presenting content developed by others without either attribution or without permission, or
- otherwise misleading consumers, including use of misleading images. *(Adopted 1/07, Amended 1/18)*

- Standard of Practice 12-11

REALTORS® intending to share or sell consumer information gathered via the Internet shall disclose that possibility in a reasonable and readily apparent manner. *(Adopted 1/07)*

- Standard of Practice 12-12

REALTORS® shall not:

- use URLs or domain names that present less than a true picture, or
- register URLs or domain names which, if used, would present less than a true picture. *(Adopted 1/08)*

- Standard of Practice 12-13

The obligation to present a true picture in advertising, marketing, and representations allows REALTORS® to use and display only professional designations, certifications, and other credentials to which they are legitimately entitled. *(Adopted 1/08)*

Article 13 (Case Interpretations for Article 13)

REALTORS® shall not engage in activities that constitute the unauthorized practice of law and shall recommend that legal counsel be obtained when the interest of any party to the transaction requires it.

Article 14 (Case Interpretations for Article 14)

If charged with unethical practice or asked to present evidence or to cooperate in any other way, in any professional standards proceeding or investigation, REALTORS® shall place all pertinent facts before the proper tribunals of the Member Board or affiliated institute, society, or council in which membership is held and shall take no action to disrupt or obstruct such processes. *(Amended 1/99)*

- Standard of Practice 14-1

REALTORS® shall not be subject to disciplinary proceedings in more than one Board of REALTORS® or affiliated institute, society or council in which they hold membership with respect to alleged violations of the Code of Ethics relating to the same transaction or event. *(Amended 1/95)*

- Standard of Practice 14-2

REALTORS® shall not make any unauthorized disclosure or dissemination of the allegations, findings, or decision developed in connection with an ethics hearing or appeal or in connection with an arbitration hearing or procedural review. *(Amended 1/92)*

- Standard of Practice 14-3

REALTORS® shall not obstruct the Board's investigative or professional standards proceedings by instituting or threatening to institute actions for libel, slander or defamation against any party to a professional standards proceeding or their witnesses based on the filing of an arbitration request, an ethics complaint, or testimony given before any tribunal. *(Adopted 11/87, Amended 1/99)*

- Standard of Practice 14-4

REALTORS® shall not intentionally impede the Board's investigative or disciplinary proceedings by filing multiple ethics complaints based on the same event or transaction. *(Adopted 11/88)*

Duties to REALTORS®

Article 15 (Case Interpretations for Article 15)

REALTORS® shall not knowingly or recklessly make false or misleading statements about other real estate professionals, their businesses, or their business practices. *(Amended 1/12)*

- Standard of Practice 15-1

REALTORS® shall not knowingly or recklessly file false or unfounded ethics complaints. *(Adopted 1/00)*

- Standard of Practice 15-2

The obligation to refrain from making false or misleading statements about other real estate professionals, their businesses and their business practices includes the duty to not knowingly or recklessly publish, repeat, retransmit, or republish false or misleading statements made by others. This duty applies whether false or misleading statements are repeated in person, in writing, by technological means (e.g., the Internet), or by any other means. *(Adopted 1/07, Amended 1/12)*

- Standard of Practice 15-3

The obligation to refrain from making false or misleading statements about other real estate professionals, their businesses, and their business practices includes the duty to publish a clarification about or to remove statements made by others on electronic media the REALTOR® controls once the

REALTOR® knows the statement is false or misleading. *(Adopted 1/10, Amended 1/12)*

Article 16 (Case Interpretations for Article 16)

REALTORS® shall not engage in any practice or take any action inconsistent with exclusive representation or exclusive brokerage relationship agreements that other REALTORS® have with clients. *(Amended 1/04)*

- Standard of Practice 16-1

Article 16 is not intended to prohibit aggressive or innovative business practices which are otherwise ethical and does not prohibit disagreements with other REALTORS® involving commission, fees, compensation or other forms of payment or expenses. *(Adopted 1/93, Amended 1/95)*

- Standard of Practice 16-2

Article 16 does not preclude REALTORS® from making general announcements to prospects describing their services and the terms of their availability even though some recipients may have entered into agency agreements or other exclusive relationships with another REALTOR®. A general telephone canvass, general mailing or distribution addressed to all prospects in a given geographical area or in a given profession, business, club, or organization, or other classification or group is deemed "general" for purposes of this standard. *(Amended 1/04)*

Article 16 is intended to recognize as unethical two basic types of solicitations:

First, telephone or personal solicitations of property owners who have been identified by a real estate sign, multiple listing compilation, or other information service as having exclusively listed their property with another REALTOR®, and

Second, mail or other forms of written solicitations of prospects whose properties are exclusively listed with another REALTOR® when such solicitations are not part of a general mailing but are directed specifically to property owners identified through compilations of current listings, "for sale" or "for rent" signs, or other sources of information required by Article 3 and Multiple Listing Service rules to be made available to other REALTORS® under offers of subagency or cooperation. *(Amended 1/04)*

- Standard of Practice 16-3

Article 16 does not preclude REALTORS® from contacting the client of another broker for the purpose of offering to provide, or entering into a contract to provide, a different type of real estate service unrelated to the type of service currently being provided (e.g., property management as opposed to brokerage) or from offering the same type of service for property not subject to other brokers' exclusive agreements. However, information received through a Multiple Listing Service or any other offer of cooperation may not be used to target clients of other REALTORS® to whom such offers to provide services may be made. *(Amended 1/04)*

- Standard of Practice 16-4

REALTORS® shall not solicit a listing which is currently listed exclusively with another broker. However, if the listing broker, when asked by the REALTOR®, refuses to disclose the expiration date and nature of such listing; i.e., an exclusive right to sell, an exclusive agency, open listing, or other form of contractual agreement between the listing broker and the client, the REALTOR® may contact the owner to secure such information and may discuss the terms upon which the REALTOR® might take a future listing or, alternatively, may take a listing to become effective upon expiration of any existing exclusive listing. *(Amended 1/94)*

- Standard of Practice 16-5

REALTORS® shall not solicit buyer/tenant agreements from buyers/ tenants who are subject to exclusive buyer/tenant agreements. However, if asked by a REALTOR®, the broker refuses to disclose the expiration date of the exclusive buyer/tenant agreement, the REALTOR® may contact the buyer/tenant to secure such information and may discuss the terms upon which the REALTOR® might enter into a future buyer/tenant agreement or, alternatively, may enter into a buyer/tenant agreement to become effective upon the expiration of any existing exclusive buyer/tenant agreement. *(Adopted 1/94, Amended 1/98)*

- Standard of Practice 16-6

When REALTORS® are contacted by the client of another REALTOR® regarding the creation of an exclusive relationship to provide the same type of service, and REALTORS® have not directly or indirectly initiated such discussions, they may discuss the terms upon which they might enter into a future agreement or, alternatively, may enter into an agreement which becomes effective upon expiration of any existing exclusive agreement. *(Amended 1/98)*

- Standard of Practice 16-7

The fact that a prospect has retained a REALTOR® as an exclusive representative or exclusive broker in one or more past transactions does not preclude other REALTORS® from seeking such prospect's future business. *(Amended 1/04)*

- Standard of Practice 16-8

The fact that an exclusive agreement has been entered into with a REALTOR® shall not preclude or inhibit any other REALTOR® from entering into a similar agreement after the expiration of the prior agreement. *(Amended 1/98)*

- Standard of Practice 16-9

REALTORS®, prior to entering into a representation agreement, have an affirmative obligation to make reasonable efforts to determine whether the prospect is subject to a current, valid exclusive agreement to provide the same type of real estate service. *(Amended 1/04)*

- Standard of Practice 16-10

REALTORS®, acting as buyer or tenant representatives or brokers, shall disclose that relationship to the seller/landlord's representative or broker at first contact and shall provide written confirmation of that disclosure to the seller/landlord's representative or broker not later than execution of a purchase agreement or lease. *(Amended 1/04)*

- Standard of Practice 16-11

On unlisted property, REALTORS® acting as buyer/tenant representatives or brokers shall disclose that relationship to the seller/landlord at first contact for that buyer/tenant and shall provide written confirmation of such disclosure to the seller/landlord not later than execution of any purchase or lease agreement. *(Amended 1/04)*

REALTORS® shall make any request for anticipated compensation from the seller/ landlord at first contact. *(Amended 1/98)*

- Standard of Practice 16-12

REALTORS®, acting as representatives or brokers of sellers/landlords or as subagents of listing brokers, shall disclose that relationship to buyers/tenants as soon as practicable and shall provide written confirmation of such disclosure to buyers/tenants not later than execution of any purchase or lease agreement. *(Amended 1/04)*

- Standard of Practice 16-13

All dealings concerning property exclusively listed, or with buyer/tenants who are subject to an exclusive agreement shall be carried on with the client's representative or broker, and not with the client, except with the consent of the client's representative or broker or except where such dealings are initiated by the client.

Before providing substantive services (such as writing a purchase offer or presenting a CMA) to prospects, REALTORS® shall ask prospects whether they are a party to any exclusive representation agreement. REALTORS® shall not knowingly provide substantive services concerning a prospective transaction to prospects who are parties to exclusive representation agreements, except with the consent of the prospects' exclusive representatives or at the direction of prospects. *(Adopted 1/93, Amended 1/04)*

- Standard of Practice 16-14

REALTORS® are free to enter into contractual relationships or to negotiate with sellers/ landlords, buyers/tenants or others who are not subject to an exclusive agreement but shall not knowingly obligate them to pay more than one commission except with their informed consent. *(Amended 1/98)*

- Standard of Practice 16-15

In cooperative transactions REALTORS® shall compensate cooperating REALTORS® (principal brokers) and shall not compensate nor offer to compensate, directly or indirectly, any of the sales licensees employed by or affiliated with other REALTORS® without the prior express knowledge and consent of the cooperating broker.

- Standard of Practice 16-16

REALTORS®, acting as subagents or buyer/tenant representatives or brokers, shall not use the terms of an offer to purchase/lease to attempt to modify the listing broker's offer of compensation to subagents or buyer/tenant representatives or brokers nor make the submission of an executed offer to purchase/lease contingent on the listing broker's agreement to modify the offer of compensation. *(Amended 1/04)*

- Standard of Practice 16-17

REALTORS®, acting as subagents or as buyer/tenant representatives or brokers, shall not attempt to extend a listing broker's offer of cooperation and/or compensation to other brokers without the consent of the listing broker. *(Amended 1/04)*

- Standard of Practice 16-18

REALTORS® shall not use information obtained from listing brokers through offers to cooperate made through multiple listing services or through other offers of cooperation to refer listing brokers' clients to other brokers or to create buyer/tenant relationships with listing brokers' clients, unless such use is authorized by listing brokers. *(Amended 1/02)*

- Standard of Practice 16-19

Signs giving notice of property for sale, rent, lease, or exchange shall not be placed on property without consent of the seller/landlord. *(Amended 1/93)*

- Standard of Practice 16-20

REALTORS®, prior to or after their relationship with their current firm is terminated, shall not induce clients of their current firm to cancel exclusive contractual agreements between the client and that firm. This does not preclude REALTORS® (principals) from establishing agreements with their associated licensees governing assignability of exclusive agreements. *(Adopted 1/98, Amended 1/10)*

Article 17 (Case Interpretations for Article 17)

In the event of contractual disputes or specific non-contractual disputes as defined in Standard of Practice 17-4 between REALTORS® (principals) associated with different firms, arising out of their relationship as REALTORS®, the REALTORS® shall mediate the dispute if the Board requires its members to mediate. If the dispute is not resolved through mediation, or if mediation is not required, REALTORS® shall submit the dispute to arbitration in accordance with the policies of their Board rather than litigate the matter.

In the event clients of REALTORS® wish to mediate or arbitrate contractual disputes arising out of real estate transactions, REALTORS® shall mediate or arbitrate those disputes in accordance with the policies of the Board, provided the clients agree to be bound by any resulting agreement or award.

The obligation to participate in mediation or arbitration contemplated by this Article includes the obligation of REALTORS® (principals) to cause their firms to mediate or arbitrate and be bound by any resulting agreement or award. *(Amended 1/12)*

- Standard of Practice 17-1

The filing of litigation and refusal to withdraw from it by REALTORS® in an arbitrable matter constitutes a refusal to arbitrate. *(Adopted 2/86)*

- Standard of Practice 17-2

Article 17 does not require REALTORS® to mediate in those circumstances when all parties to the dispute advise the Board in writing that they choose not to mediate through the Board's facilities. The fact that all parties decline to participate in mediation does not relieve REALTORS® of the duty to arbitrate.

Article 17 does not require REALTORS® to arbitrate in those circumstances when all parties to the dispute advise the Board in writing that they choose not to arbitrate before the Board. *(Amended 1/12)*

- Standard of Practice 17-3

REALTORS®, when acting solely as principals in a real estate transaction, are not obligated to arbitrate disputes with other REALTORS® absent a specific written agreement to the contrary. *(Adopted 1/96)*

- Standard of Practice 17-4

Specific non-contractual disputes that are subject to arbitration pursuant to Article 17 are:

- Where a listing broker has compensated a cooperating broker and another cooperating broker subsequently claims to be the procuring cause of the sale or lease. In such cases the complainant may name the first cooperating broker as respondent and arbitration may proceed without the listing broker being named as a respondent. When arbitration occurs between two (or more) cooperating brokers and where the listing broker is not a party, the amount in dispute and the amount of any potential resulting award is limited to the amount paid to the respondent by the listing broker and any amount credited or paid to a party to the transaction at the direction of the respondent. Alternatively, if the complaint is brought against the listing broker, the listing broker may name the first cooperating broker as a third-party respondent. In either instance the decision of the hearing panel as to procuring cause shall be conclusive with respect to all current or subsequent claims of the parties for compensation arising out of the underlying cooperative transaction. *(Adopted 1/97, Amended 1/07)*

- Where a buyer or tenant representative is compensated by the seller or landlord, and not by the listing broker, and the listing broker, as a result, reduces the commission owed by the seller or landlord and, subsequent to such actions, another cooperating broker claims to be the procuring cause of sale or lease. In such cases the complainant may name the first cooperating broker as respondent and arbitration may proceed without the listing broker being named as a respondent. When arbitration occurs between two (or more) cooperating brokers and where the listing broker is not a party, the amount in dispute and the amount of any potential resulting award is limited to the amount paid to the respondent by the seller or landlord and any amount credited or paid to a party to the transaction at the direction of the respondent. Alternatively, if the complaint is brought against the listing broker, the listing broker may name the first cooperating broker as a third-party respondent. In either instance the decision of the hearing panel as to procuring cause shall be conclusive with respect to all current or subsequent claims of the parties for compensation arising out of the underlying cooperative transaction. *(Adopted 1/97, Amended 1/07)*

- Where a buyer or tenant representative is compensated by the buyer or tenant and, as a result, the listing broker reduces the commission owed by the seller or landlord and, subsequent to such actions, another cooperating broker claims to be the procuring cause of sale or lease. In such cases the complainant may name the first cooperating broker as respondent and arbitration may proceed without the listing broker being named as a respondent. Alternatively, if the complaint is brought against the listing broker, the listing broker may name the first cooperating broker as a third-party respondent. In either instance the decision of the hearing panel as to procuring cause shall be conclusive with respect to all current or subsequent claims of the parties for compensation arising out of the underlying cooperative transaction. *(Adopted 1/97)*

- Where two or more listing brokers claim entitlement to compensation pursuant to open listings with a seller or landlord who agrees to participate in arbitration (or who requests arbitration) and who agrees to be bound by the decision. In cases where one of the listing brokers has been compensated by the seller or landlord, the other listing broker, as complainant, may name the first listing broker as respondent and arbitration may proceed between the brokers. *(Adopted 1/97)*
- Where a buyer or tenant representative is compensated by the seller or landlord, and not by the listing broker, and the listing broker, as a result, reduces the commission owed by the seller or landlord and, subsequent to such actions, claims to be the procuring cause of sale or lease. In such cases arbitration shall be between the listing broker and the buyer or tenant representative and the amount in dispute is limited to the amount of the reduction of commission to which the listing broker agreed. *(Adopted 1/05)*
- Standard of Practice 17-5

The obligation to arbitrate established in Article 17 includes disputes between REALTORS® (principals) in different states in instances where, absent an established inter–association arbitration agreement, the REALTOR® (principal) requesting arbitration agrees to submit to the jurisdiction of, travel to, participate in, and be bound by any resulting award rendered in arbitration conducted by the respondent(s) REALTOR®'s association, in instances where the respondent(s) REALTOR®'s association determines that an arbitrable issue exists. *(Adopted 1/07)*

Explanatory Notes

The reader should be aware of the following policies which have been approved by the Board of Directors of the National Association:

In filing a charge of an alleged violation of the Code of Ethics by a REALTOR®, the charge must read as an alleged violation of one or more Articles of the Code. Standards of Practice may be cited in support of the charge.

The Standards of Practice serve to clarify the ethical obligations imposed by the various Articles and supplement, and do not substitute for, the Case Interpretations in Interpretations of the Code of Ethics.

Modifications to existing Standards of Practice and additional new Standards of Practice are approved from time to time. Readers are cautioned to ensure that the most recent publications are utilized.

NOTES

www.ingramcontent.com/pod-product-compliance
Lightning Source LLC
LaVergne TN
LVHW052027080426
835513LV00018B/2212
* 9 7 8 0 5 7 8 8 9 2 4 9 8 *